CAMPAIGN 389

THE HYDASPES 326 BC

The Limit of Alexander the Great's Conquests

NIC FIELDS

ILLUSTRATED BY MARCO CAPPARONI

Series editor Nikolai Bogdanovic

OSPREY PUBLISHING
Bloomsbury Publishing Plc
Kemp House, Chawley Park, Cumnor Hill, Oxford OX2 9PH, UK
29 Earlsfort Terrace, Dublin 2, Ireland
1385 Broadway, 5th Floor, New York, NY 10018, USA
E-mail: info@ospreypublishing.com
www.ospreypublishing.com

OSPREY is a trademark of Osprey Publishing Ltd

First published in Great Britain in 2023

A catalogue record for this book is available from the British Library.

ISBN: PB 9781472853905; eBook 9781472853912; ePDF 9781472853899;
XML 9781472853882

23 24 25 26 27 10 9 8 7 6 5 4 3 2 1

Maps by Bounford.com
3D BEVs by Paul Kime
Index by Zoe Ross
Typeset by PDQ Digital Media Solutions, Bungay, UK
Printed and bound in India by Replika Press Private Ltd.

Artist's note

Readers may care to note that the original paintings from which the colour
plates in this book were prepared are available for private sale. All
reproduction copyright whatsoever is retained by the publishers. All
enquiries should be addressed to the artist via the below website:

https://marcocapparoni.com/

The publishers regret that they can enter into no correspondence upon
this matter.

Osprey Publishing supports the Woodland Trust, the UK's leading woodland
conservation charity.

To find out more about our authors and books visit
www.ospreypublishing.com. Here you will find extracts, author
interviews, details of forthcoming events and the option to sign up for
our newsletter.

Key to military symbols

XXXXX	XXXX	XXX	XX	X	III	II
Army Group	Army	Corps	Division	Brigade	Regiment	Battalion

				Key to unit identification
I		•	◣	
Company/Battery	Infantry	Artillery	Cavalry	

Key to unit identification

Unit identifier — Parent unit

Commander

(+) with added elements
(−) less elements

Title page: Detail from the *Alexander Mosaic* (Napoli, Museo
archeologico nazionale) from the Casa del Fauno, Pompeii (VI, 12, 2),
showing Alexander in battle at the moment when he leads a charge
pell-mell into the heart of the Persian array. (Berthold Werner/
Wikimedia Commons/Public domain)

Front cover main illustration: Alexander and his men overcome an
Indian mobile force of chariots and horsemen led by one of Poros'
sons in the first encounter of the battle of the Hydaspes. (Marco
Capparoni)

CONTENTS

Before the fall: the Achaemenid empire

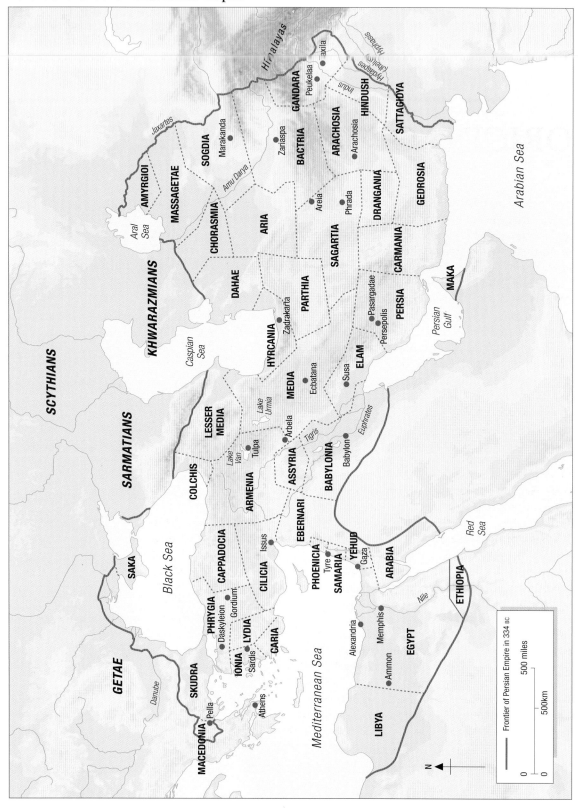

Himalayas
Jaxartes
Taxila
GANDARA
Peukelaa
HINDUSH
Hydaspes (Jhelum)
Hyphasis
Indus
SOGDIA
Marakanda
Zariaspa
BACTRIA
ARACHOSIA
Zariaspa
SATTAGYDIA
AMYRGIOI
MASSAGETAE
Amu Darya
Areia
Phrada
ARACHOSIA
Arachosia
GEDROSIA
Areia
CHORASMIA
ARIA
DRANGANIA
Aral Sea
DAHAE
SAGARTIA
CARMANIA
MAKA
KHWARAZMIANS
PARTHIA
Pasargadae
Zadrakarta
Pasargadae
Persepolis
PERSIA
Arabian Sea
Caspian Sea
HYRCANIA
ELAM
Persian Gulf
SCYTHIANS
MEDIA
Susa
Ecbatana
Arbela
SARMATIANS
LESSER MEDIA
Lake Urmia
Tigris
Euphrates
Lake Van
Tulpa
ASSYRIA
BABYLONIA
Babylon
COLCHIS
ARMENIA
EBERNARI
Red Sea
SAKA
CAPPADOCIA
Issus
YEHUD
Black Sea
CILICIA
PHOENICIA
Gaza
ARABIA
PHRYGIA
Daskyleion
Gordium
Tyre
SAMARIA
ETHIOPIA
GETAE
IONIA
LYDIA
CARIA
Nile
Sardis
Alexandria
Memphis
SKUDRA
Mediterranean Sea
EGYPT
Danube
Pella
MACEDONIA
Athens
Ammon
LIBYA

N

Frontier of Persian Empire in 334 BC

500 miles
500km
0
0

ORIGINS OF THE CAMPAIGN

The victory of Alexander at Gaugamela on 1 October 331 BC was a stunning upset. After the young Macedonian king and his famed companions pierced and shattered the heart of Dareios' battle line upon the flat, dust-laden plain of northern Mesopotamia, the Great King fled the field post-haste, destined never again to offer significant resistance to the western invaders. For nearly three years, Alexander and his army of professional Macedonian and Greek soldiers had won a series of climatic victories against the Achaemenid Persians, the ancient enemies of the Greeks. By doing so, they had 'spear-won' the lands of Anatolia, the Levant, and Egypt and added them to the rapidly expanding Macedonian landblock of an empire. Though he was outnumbered considerably – Dareios had drawn his army from every corner of his vast empire eastwards – Alexander won his most decisive victory at Gaugamela, which opened the rest of the crumbling Persian domains to conquest.

Though this victory at Gaugamela assured Alexander of mastery over the rubble of the Persian empire, which had been the largest and most multinational empire known at the time, his ambitions did not stop there. Over the next seven years, Alexander and his army fought a messy but truly Herculean series of campaigns in what are today Iran, Turkmenistan, Afghanistan, and Pakistan. It is the last locality, the Indus Valley to be precise, which is the matter of interest in this monograph. It was here, on the left bank of the Hydaspes (Jhelum) River, the Vitastā of Sanskrit texts (e.g. RV 10.75), that Alexander fought his last great (and most costly) pitched battle as he advanced from Taxila (Takshiçila, near Islamabad) to invade the Indian Subcontinent. Additionally, on that day he was to face a worthy opponent under exceptional circumstances.

'Let him read and meditate on the wars of the great commanders; that is the only way to learn about war,' runs one of the myriad quotes of Napoleon recorded while he was in gloomy exile on Saint Helena. On the subject of leadership, the victorious general par excellence had much to say, of course. He had certainly made a deep study of Alexander's campaigns and learned from them. At the pivotal battle of Wagram (4–6 July 1809) Napoleon faced a comparable problem on the Danube that Alexander had faced on the Hydaspes, and solved it the same way: Napoleon kept a pinning force across from the Austrian camp, despatched a turning force upriver, crossed onto an island, and turned the Austrian flank – all during frequent squalls of rain and a series of violent thunderstorms. Many commentators place Wagram among Napoleon's greatest battles in terms of tactical skill. Some

Detail from the *Alexander Mosaic* (Napoli, Museo archeologico nazionale) from the Casa del Fauno, Pompeii (VI, 12, 2). Unearthed in 1831, the vast floor mosaic (3.13 x 5.82m) is thought to be a Roman copy (*c*. 120/100 BC) of an original painting by Philoxenos of Eretria produced in (or very shortly after) the lifetime of Alexander (Plin. 35.110). The detail depicts Alexander in battle at the moment when he leads a charge pell-mell into the heart of the Persian array. Alexander is wearing a composite *linothōrax* with metal shoulder and chest pieces (bronze or iron) but midriff of overlapping metal scales for flexibility – on a number of occasions he is noted for 'the [Homeric] splendour of his panoply' (Arr. *Anab*. 1.14.4, 6.9.5, cf. Curt. 4.4.11). He is riding his Thessalian horse Boukephálas, who would die after the Hydaspes either from age and exhaustion (Plut. *Alex*. 61, Arr. *Anab*. 5.19.4, cf. 14.4) or of fatal injuries (Strab. 15.1.29, *Metz Epit*. 62, Curt. 8.14.34). The devoted old warhorse was apparently aged upwards of 30 years and was buried on the banks of the Hydaspes (Plut. *Alex*. 61, Arr. *Anab*. 5.20.1-2). The mosaic is traditionally believed to depict Issos, but in reality its theme better fits Gaugamela, the day Alexander consigned the Achaemenid empire to history and he became the Great King. (Berthold Werner/ Wikimedia Commons/ Public domain)

ten years earlier, when Alexander's campaigns were being read to the young Napoleon during his Egyptian campaign, it was the battle of the Hydaspes that particularly caught his admirer's attention: not as all-encompassing as the dramatic and decisive encounter at Gaugamela, it was a good deal subtler and more indirect in its approach than anything seen in the arena of warfare before. Depending on shrewdness, surprise, speed and skill, this last set-piece battle would be the young Macedonian king at his very best.

LITERARY SOURCES

Although some half a dozen or so of his contemporaries chronicled Alexander's life and campaigns, much of these texts have perished without trace. Enough remains, however, in the shape of fragments embedded in extant writers. The fragments (Kallisthenēs of Olynthos *FGrHist* 124, Anaximenes of Lampsakos *FGrHist* 72 FF15–17, 29, Onēsikritos of Astypalaia *FGrHist* 134, Nearkhos of Crete *FGrHist* 133, Ptolemaios son of Lagos *FGrHist* 138, Aristoboulos of Kassandreia (formerly Potidaia) *FGrHist* 139 F55, F56, Kleitarkhos of Alexandria *FGrHist* 137) indicate that the original texts by these actors or observers who followed in Alexander's footsteps offered widely diverse views of both the achievements and morality of Alexander. Many letters and speeches attributed to Alexander are cited in our sources, but they are ancient forgeries or reconstructions inspired by quixotic imagination or political motives. The little solid documentation we possess from Alexander's own time is mainly to be found in the mere handful of inscriptions from the Greek *poleis* of Europe and Asia that can be dated with reasonable confidence to that period (Austin 5, Harding 102, 105–7, 110, 112A, 113–14, 122).

Regrettably, the original tradition of Alexander's reign is only accessible through the distorting filter of the extant sources composed between 300 and 500 years after Alexander's death. That means in practice five primary authorities: Diodoros Siculus (*c*. 80–20 BC), Quintus Curtius Rufus (d. AD 53), Plutarch (*fl*. AD 100), Lucius (or Aulus) Flavius Arrianus (*fl*. AD 130),

and Justinus' epitome of the *Historiae Philippicae* by the polymath Cnaeus Pompeius Trogus (*fl.* 20 BC). To these we might add an obscure epitome of a history of Alexander contained in a single manuscript from Metz. Surviving as two 19th-century transcriptions (the original was destroyed in a bombing raid during World War II), the *Metz Epitome* is a peculiar work that begins with the death of Dareios III and ends, abruptly, with Alexander's descent of the Indus. It has much in common with Curtius and Justinus-Trogus, as well as the occasional resemblance to Diodoros Siculus.

Regarding the reliability of the five non-contemporary historians apropos Alexander, as Elizabeth Baynham remarks: 'One needs to exercise caution … ancient authors often pass on statements of others without reading the work for themselves' (Roisman 2003: 8).

Arrianus was a Greek historian and philosopher from Nikomēdeia, the capital of the Roman province of Bithynia. As his father or grandfather had been granted Roman citizenship, probably by one of the Flavian emperors (AD 69–96), Arrianus was able to take a career in imperial service. His imperial advancement was rapid, and in AD 129 or AD 130 he achieved the consulship. But it was his appointment as the *legatus* of the frontier province of Kappadokia from *c.* AD 132 to AD 137 that demonstrated how greatly Hadrianus (r. AD 117–38) trusted Arrianus' undoubted military and administrative abilities. With the task of protecting the upper Euphrates, his command included two legions and numerous auxiliaries, a rare responsibility for a *Graeculus*, 'Greekling', at that time. He saw action against the Alanoi, a campaign he describes in *Ektaxis kata Alanon* (*The Expedition against the Alans*).

As a conscious archaiser, Arrianus was a great admirer of Xenophon (he styled himself the 'Second Xenophon') and for our purposes Arrianus' *Anabasis Alexandri* (*The Campaigns of Alexander*) is his most important extant work. Though it remains the fullest and most reliable source on Alexander's campaigns – derived mostly from the best-informed witnesses Ptolemaios (who concerned himself largely with military and administrative matters) and Aristoboulos (who was more interested in geography and

Landscape outside Erbil (ancient Arbela), Iraqi Kurdistan. Gaugamela, which took place northwest of Arbela, was the decisive final clash between Alexander and Dareios. The exact location of the battlefield has been disputed, but it is generally accepted that it was the level plain today called Naqūr surrounding Tel Gomel, as first proposed by Aurel Stein. It was ideal for Dareios' leviathan army, which had been drawn chiefly from the east and so consisted of the best troops in his empire. Even the vast number of superb horsemen and the terrifying scythed chariots mustered on that day were not enough to overcome the confidence of Alexander's outnumbered army. On what was an extremely flat, open dusty plain, Alexander blunted all of Dareios' attacks, and then countered with a cavalry charge that caused the Great King to flee the field and his army to collapse. Dareios initially fled to Arbela, and it was here that Alexander found the baggage of the Great King. (Zirguezi/Wikimedia Commons/Public domain)

The western spur of the Himalayas known as the Hindu Kush, rising majestically behind Kabul. Military historians have agreed that as a feat of leadership and endurance Alexander's crossing of the Hindu Kush via the Khawak Pass (elev. 3,848m) in the early spring of 329 BC far surpasses Hannibal's celebrated crossing of the Alps. The Macedonian army struggled through snow drifts and biting winds, and suffered from chronic fatigue, snow blindness and altitude sickness. Often, the only thing that kept it moving was their king's indefatigable willpower. The usual time for crossing the 76km-pass was four days, but for the large numbers of men and animals that made up the army and a degree of physical exhaustion induced by the terrain, their harrowing journey was to take four times as long (Strab. 15.2.10, 15 days; Diod. 17.83.1, 16 days; Curt. 7.3.21, 17 days). Though for 2,500 years Afghanistan was always part of some outsider's empire, beginning with the Achaemenid Persians, no foreign invader had ever dared such a feat before with so many, and no one ever would again, not even the Soviets. (Davric/Wikimedia Commons/ Public domain)

natural history) – we do need to allow for the inaccuracies and omissions. As Paul Goukowsky observes, 'the Ptolemaic founder wrote an uncritical history of a conqueror with no weaknesses' (1978: 144). This Alexander was to conquer Arrianus. For the Hydaspes, see *Anabasis* 5.8.4–15.2 (background), and 5.15.3–19.3 (battle).

The *Historiae Alexandri Magni Macedonis* of **Curtius** originally comprised ten books and was thus the only full-length account of the Macedonian conqueror written in Latin. Unfortunately, there are a number of *lacunae*: the first two books are lost, as are the end of Book 5 and beginning of Book 6, as well as significant portions of Book 10. Curtius seems to have taken Livy as his model, just as Arrianus took Xenophon for his.

Curtius has much to say about the corrupting nature of power, and so depicts Alexander in his latter years as an oriental despot, almost a vindictive, ruthless tyrant whose model was either Caius or Nero, both of whom executed senators in his own lifetime. Indeed, his work is full of rhetorical narratives but preserves many traditions from the side of the Persians. For the Hydaspes, see 8.13.5–14.

Diodoros Siculus was a Greek historian who was born at Argyrion (Agira) on the island of Sicily. He wrote a *Bibliothēkē* (*Universal History*) of the Mediterranean world in 40 books (15 of which are extant) from the earliest times to the period of Caesar's conquest of Gaul – he was a contemporary of Caesar and Augustus. Although he is somewhat dull at times and often untrustworthy, his work is extremely useful in that it provides an alternative tradition of events. Moreover, his value lies in the fact that he clearly based his work on earlier historians whose texts have not survived (e.g. Ephoros, Hieronymos of Kardia) or have survived only in small fragments (e.g. Timaios). Book 17 is assigned to Alexander's campaigns: for the Hydaspes, see 17.87.1–89.3, though he fails to mention the crucial river crossing.

Plutarch, from Chairōneia in Boiotia, was a Greek who moved in the cultured Roman circles of his day, and may have held some imperial posts under the emperors Traianus and Hadrianus. Educated in Athens, Plutarch was an eclectic philosopher, essayist and biographer. He was also a member

Obverse of silver *tetradrachm* (Paris, Cabinet des Médailles, inv. FG M2157) with a posthumous portrait of Alexander, issued by Ptolemaios I Sōtēr (r. 305–282 BC). Alexander is depicted in a radical new pose wearing an Indian elephant scalp headdress, perhaps recalling the Hydaspes in which both men had fought. Ptolemaios (b. 367 BC) was a companion of Alexander who wrote an eyewitness account (now lost) of Alexander's campaigns: Arrianus once named Ptolemaios as the author 'whom I chiefly follow' (*Anab.* 6.2.4), high praise indeed, though Curtius stated that Ptolemaios had 'no desire to detract from his own reputation' (9.5.21), and modern commentators tend to accuse Ptolemaios of blatant self-promotion. He hijacked Alexander's embalmed remains, which he initially entombed at Memphis (321 BC), the old capital of the pharaohs, later transferring the corpse to Alexandria, where the magnificent tomb of Parian marble was the focus of funeral games (Curt. 10.10.20, Paus. 1.6.3). By doing so, the then satrap of Egypt placed himself under the protection of the 'god' Alexander, and helped to create the Alexander myth. One of the giants of the tumultuous age of the Diadochoi, it is said Ptolemaios would blush when asked the name of his grandmother (it was rumoured he was a bastard son of Philip), but he died a pharaoh of Egypt. (Marie-Lan Nguyen/Wikimedia Commons/CC-BY-SA-2.5)

of the college of priests at Delphi. His *Bíoi parálleloi* (*Parallel Lives*) are an extremely useful, although late, source for Greek (and Roman) history as he collected much detail and various traditions. However, Plutarch is well known for focalizing his heroes and so can be fairly uncritical. Although his main aim is to moralize about the nature of the man, he does make a fair stab in some of the *Lives*, which were written in pairs of Greeks and Romans of similar eminence (e.g. Alexander and Iulius Caesar, Demosthenes and Cicero), at producing some sort of history. It should be noted that Plutarch pays more attention to the evolution of Alexander's behaviour during the course of his succession of almost continuous campaigns than he ever does in his other didactic biographies, so revealing to us the shadows that increase in density as the campaign of conquest proceeds.

Plutarch's vast output outside the *Lives* is collectively known as the *Moralia* (*Moral Essays*) and includes some interesting pieces on questions of personal conduct. Again, Plutarch presents a young king full of the right virtues who gradually turns into an implacable despot. Plutarch (*Alex.* 27.5, 39.6, 41.3–4, 42.1) infers that he saw or possessed letters from Alexander himself, and for the Hydaspes he says, 'Of his campaigns against Poros he himself has given an account in his letters' (*Alex.* 60.1). However, we cannot be sure that Plutarch could always distinguish the genuine from the spurious. Besides, as J.R. Hamilton says: 'Plutarch, even if the letter of Alexander on which he bases his account is genuine, treats the battle itself in too summary a fashion to be of much value' (1956: 26).

Bas-relief, external gallery, main temple of Angkor Wat, Cambodia. The largest religious monument in the world, Angkor Wat was originally a Hindu centre of worship – it was dedicated to the supreme god Viṣṇu – which is reflected in its bas-reliefs. This one depicts a scene from the *Mahābhārata* showing *kṣatriyas* engaged in battle: *kṣatriya*, the second highest in ritual status of the four *varṇas* of Hindu society, traditionally the warrior aristocracy. In the *Arthaśāstra* they were 'protectors of the land' (14.3.35), while the *Mahābhārata* says 'among men the highest duties are those performed by the *kṣatriyas*' (12.63.24). And the true spirit of the warrior's duty lies in the pursuit of arms (San. *śastrājīva*), no matter what. In the *Bhagavad Gītā* (2.31–3) Krishna elaborates a view of duty and action intended to convince Arjuna that, as a *kṣatriya*, he must overcome all his doubts and take up arms, even against his own relatives. (Marcin Konsek/Wikimedia Commons/ CC-BY-SA-4.0)

The *Arthaśāstra* of **Kauṭilya** contains the most complete account of Hindu ideas on politics, economics, law and war. However, we are faced with the intricate problem of date: the *Arthaśāstra* was supposedly compiled between the 4th and 3rd centuries BC, while Indian tradition presupposes that the author helped the future conqueror Chandragupta Maurya become the raja of Magadha. There is, however, no doubt that Chandragupta ascended the throne around 321 BC and was to be the first conqueror to join together the Indus Valley and the Gangetic Plain in one extensive empire.

Whatever may be its actual date, the *Arthaśāstra* compresses within itself a vast mass of useful information regarding the art of warfare of the ancient Indians. It describes the compositions of the army and the relative value of its four elements. It speaks of the duties of the various military officers, and defines the functions of the different elements. This monumental Indian text on statecraft and strategy contains information on the training of horses and elephants, for marching, encamping, fortifications, siegecraft, espionage and much else besides.

The *Mahābhārata* is reckoned to be some 3,500 years old, though the bulk of the text was probably compiled between the 3rd century BC and the 3rd century AD, reaching its final form in the following century. As P.C. Chakravarti justly observed: 'For the epics, especially the *Mahābhārata*, represent a veritable museum in which the relics of different ages have been stored in a hopelessly ill-sorted and confused manner' (2017: iii). Eventually running to a shade less than 80,000 Sanskrit *shlokas* or verse stanzas (some 2 million words), it is the longest composition in existence: roughly ten times the length of the *Iliad* and the *Odyssey* combined. Traditionally, the authorship of the *Mahābhārata* is attributed to the legendary *brāhmaṇa* Vyāsadeva, so named because he classified (*vyāsa*) the Vedas. He is also a main character in the epic. It also contains the best-known and most famous texts of Hindu philosophy, the *Bhagavad Gītā*, the advice of Lord Krishna to the Pāṇḍava prince Arjuna, who is unmatched in the knowledge of weapons and the world's greatest archer, on the battlefield (*Mbh* 6.23–40).

The *Mahābhārata* bas-relief panel depicting the Kurukṣetra ('the field of the Kurus') war fought between the Kauravas and the Pāṇḍavas, Cave 16, Kailāśanāth rock-cut Hindu temple, Ellora Caves. Though the temple's construction is generally attributed to the Rāṣṭrakūṭa raja Krishna I (r. AD 756–74), and despite the absence of horsemen, this relief does give a very good impression of the classical Indian 'fourfold' army fielded by Poros at the Hydaspes. The *Mahābhārata* tells of heroic battles in the remote Indian past between mighty warrior rajas and their followers, fighting alongside the Hindu gods; at the Hydaspes Poros himself appeared like an avatar of one of those distant heroic champions. (Ms Sarah Welch/Wikimedia Commons/ CC-BY-SA-4.0)

Set in the northernmost part of India, the vast Hindu epic centres around the tension between two branches of a ruling family of the *kṣatriya*, warrior *varṇa*, who find they cannot share power, and an 18-day battle that ensued to settle the question of supremacy. A tale of heroism, persecution, and intrigue, the *Mahābhārata* employs the 'story within a story' format. It has plots and subplots and meanderings and digressions. The cast of characters is huge. While the original events related by the epic probably fall between the 9th and 8th centuries BC, the period of the Iron Age, much like the *Iliad* and the *Odyssey*, the *Mahābhārata* has lasted because it has something to say. Sure, it is a story told countless times before, and over the centuries it was likely to have been erratically added to, but the *Mahābhārata* offers one of our brightest windows into classical India.

Stone carving, Chennakeshava Temple at Belur, depicting Bhagadatta, riding Supratika, engaging with Bhīma on day 12 of the Kurukṣetra war. Enemy of Lord Krishna, Bhagadatta fought for the Kauravas in the *Mahābhārata*. Bhīma, the second among the five Pāṇḍavas, is wielding his weapon of choice, *Vrigodharam* ('Voracious Eater'), the huge mace whose strength is equivalent to a hundred thousand commonplace maces. On day 18 it would be the mace-fight between Bhīma and Duryodhana, the eldest Kauravas, which would decide the fate of the kingdom (*Mbh* 9.58–9). (Bhoomi/Wikimedia Commons/CC-BY-SA-3.0)

CHRONOLOGY

334 BC

Spring   Alexander crosses over the Hellespont (Dardanelles) into Asia.

Mémnōn of Rhodes advocates a scorched-earth policy (Arr. *Anab.* 1.12.9).

First victory over Persians at the Granīkos (Biga) River (Arr. *Anab.* 1.13–16, cf. the divergent account of Diod. 17.18.4–21.6).

Capture of Sardis.

Summer   Ionian *poleis* on the western seaboard of Anatolia submit to Alexander.

Re-foundation of Priene (Harding 105, 106) and Smyrna.

Fall of Miletos and Halikarnassos.

Winter   Conquests in southern Anatolia (Persian satrapies of Lycia, Pamphylia, Phrygia).

Army winters at Gordian in Phrygia.

Alexander cuts (or unravels) Gordian knot (Arr. *Anab.* 2.3, though not recorded by Diod.).

Alexander sends letter to Great King of Persia, Dareios III, in which he declares himself 'Lord of all Asia' (Arr. *Anab.* 2.14.8, cf. Plut. *Alex* 34.1)

333 BC

Spring   Alexander advances on satrapy of Cilicia.

Persians, under Mémnōn of Rhodes, counter-attack by sea, but are soundly defeated.

Summer   Death of Mémnōn.

Winter   First battle between Alexander and Dareios at Issos, Cilicia (cf. Polyb. 12.17–22, his criticisms of Kallisthenēs' account of the battle).

Defeated, Dareios flees back to Babylon abandoning the royal family to the mercy of Alexander.

Alexander subdues most of the Syro-Phoenician littoral (Byblos and Arados submit, as well as Rhodes and Cyprus, but Tyre closes its gates against him).

332 BC

Spring   Seven-month siege of Tyre – inhabitants either slain or sold into slavery.

Dareios sends letter to Alexander, offering 10,000 talents' ransom for his family, marriage alliance and territory from the Euphrates to the Aegean – Alexander rejects the offer (Arr. *Anab.* 2.25.1).

Autumn   Two-month siege of Gaza – its garrison put to the sword and 'Homeric' death of Batis, Persian commander (Curt. 4.6.29).

Winter   Unopposed entry into Egypt (Arr. *Anab.* 3.1.2, Curt. 4.7.1) – Alexander enthroned as pharaoh at Memphis.

331 BC

Spring   Foundation of Alexandria in Egypt (Arr. *Anab.* 3.1.5, Plut. *Alex.* 26.2–6, cf. Diod. 17.52.1–3, Curt. 4.8.1–2, who place this event *after* pilgrimage to Sīwah).

Expedition to oracle of Amun (Gk. Zeus Ámmōn) at desert oasis of Sīwah – greeted as son of Zeus (Diod. 17.51.3, Plut. *Alex.* 27.5, cf. Arr. *Anab.* 3.3.6, Strab. 17.43 and Kallisthenēs *FGrHist* 124 F14a, where both authors stress Alexander's desire to imitate his heroic ancestors, Heraklēs and Perseus, who had journeyed to Sīwah).

Summer   Revolt of Agis III of Sparta ('an affair of mice') sponsored by Persia (Aisch. 3.165).

March to the Euphrates at Thapsakos and unopposed entry into Mesopotamia.

March to the Tigris and unopposed entry into western Media.

Autumn Battle of Megalopolis – Antipatros defeats and kills Agis.

Winter Second battle between Alexander and Dareios at Gaugamela – Alexander makes a pan-Hellenic speech 'to the Thessalians and the other Greeks' and prays to Zeus 'to defend and strengthen the Greeks' (Plut. *Alex.* 33.1, from Kallisthenēs).

Defeated once again, Dareios, accompanied by a small retinue, flees to the eastern half of his empire.

330 BC

Spring Alexander occupies Babylon, Sousa – 'the obvious prize of the war' (Arr. *Anab.* 3.16.2) – and, after the battle at the Persian Gates, Persepolis, the ancient capital of the Persians.

Burning of palace at Persepolis (Arr. *Anab.* 3.18.11–12, cf. Diod. 17.72.1–5, Curt. 5.7.2–7, Plut. *Alex.* 38.1–8 – all following Kleitarkhos *FGrHist* 137 F11 – its destruction follows a drunken revel).

Summer Greek allies paid in full and dismissed (Arr. *Anab.* 3.19.5).

Alexander pursues Dareios, occupying satrapies of Media and Parthia.

Dareios mortally wounded by Bessos, satrap of Baktria and Dareios' kinsman, and Alexander has him buried with royal honours at Persepolis (Arr. *Anab.* 3.22.1).

Alexander assumes title 'Great King of Persia', and adopts Persian ceremonial customs and dress (Arr. *Anab.* 4.7.4, Kleitarkhos *FGrHist* 137 F5, Diod. 17.77.4, cf. Plut. *Alex.* 45.2 who claims Alexander did not take upright tiara or adopt trousers).

Autumn Parmeniōn and his eldest son Philotas accused of treason – Philotas executed; Parmeniōn murdered (Arr. *Anab.* 3.26.2–4, Curt. 6.7.1–11.40, 7.2.11–33).

Winter Alexander suppresses revolt of Satibarzanes, satrap of Areia and supporter of usurper Bessos.

329 BC

Spring After great difficulties Alexander's army crosses Hindu Kush via Khawak Pass and arrives at border of Baktria, where Bessos has established himself as Great King, taking the name of Artaxerxes (Arr. *Anab.* 3.25.3).

Foundations of Alexandria-in-Arachosia (Kandahar), Alexandria-under-the-Caucasus (Begram, near Kābul – Arr. *Anab.* 3.28.4, 4.22.5, cf. Strab. 15.2.10, Plin. 6.62), and of Alexandria-Eschatē (Khujand) on the Jaxartes (Sýr Darya) River (Arr. *Anab.* 4.1.3–4, 22.5, Curt. 7.6.25–7, Just. 12.5.12) – according to Plutarch (*Mor.* 328e, cf. Arr. *Ind.* 40.8) the 70 (Arrianus mentions fewer than a dozen) Asiatic foundations of Alexander were part-and-parcel of his Hellenizing mission, whereas Diodoros Siculus regards them, along with population transfers, as mission to bring 'common unity and common like- mindedness (*koinen homonoian*) by means of intermarriages and family ties' (18.4.4).

Summer Alexander crosses the Oxos (Amu Darya) River and enters satrapy of Baktria – waging war in Baktria like 'cutting off the heads of a hydra' (Plut. *Mor.* 341f).

Capture of Bessos by Ptolemaios and his subsequent execution at Ekbatana (Arr. *Anab.* 4.7.3, cf. Plut. *Alex.* 43.3).

Army advances on Marakanda (Samarkand).

328 BC

Summer Arduous campaign in Sogdiana (Uzbekistan-Tajikistan) – capture of Sogdian Rock.

Murder of 'Black' Kleitos at Marakanda after drunken quarrel (Arr. *Anab.* 4.8, Curt. 8.1.19–52, Plut. *Alex.* 50–1).

Treason plot against Alexander sparked by his order Macedonians perform obeisance before him ('conspiracy of the royal pages': Arr. *Anab.* 4.10–12, cf. Hdt. 1.134 for a series of graded addresses in Persian society, ranging from bow and blown kiss to complete prostration [*proskynesis*] depending on rank of subject, Plut. *Alex.* 47.5 for division among Alexander's two closest friends about his 'orientalizing').

Execution of plot's 'ringleader', court historian Kallisthenēs (kinsman and pupil of Aristotle), who had stressed publicly the importance of preserving correct distinction in honours due to gods, heroes and men, so signing his own death warrant (Arr. *Anab.* 4.11.2–3, 6–8, cf. 12.1–5 for alternative tradition on Kallisthenēs' opposition).

Winter   Alexander marries 'the most beautiful girl in Asia', Rhoxane, daughter of the Sogdian chieftain Oxyartes.

Defeat and murder of Spitamenes, last Sogdian magnate to oppose Alexander – Sakae deliver his head to Alexander's camp.

327 BC

Spring   Crossing of Hindu Kush via Bamian to Alexandria-under-the-Caucasus (Arr. *Anab.* 4.22.4).

Alexander invades north-west India.

Autumn   At the Kōphēn (Kābul) River, the army divides and proceeds in two columns to the Indus.

Alexander 'does battle' with the Indus, 'reflecting that he, like Achilles, had done battle with a river' (Diod. 17.97.3).

Winter   Punitive campaign in the Swāt Valley.

326 BC

Spring   Siege of Aornos (Pīr-Sar).

Army reunites at Udabhandapura (Hund) and crosses the Indus.

Alexander enters Taxila (Takshiçila) – encounter with Gymnosophists.

Summer   Battle of the Hydaspes (Jhelum) River – Poros wounded, defeated, captured, befriended and reinstated as raja.

Autumn   At the Hyphasis (Beās) River, where Alexander's soldiers refuse to go further, reluctantly Alexander returns to the Hydaspes (episode of the 12 gigantic altars).

Winter   Alexander defeats the 'kingless' Malloi (Mālavas) – Alexander receives near-fatal wound (Arr. *Anab.* 6.10.1) but eventually recovers.

Brāhmaṇa-led cities attacked, siege of Multān.

325 BC

Spring   Voyage down the Indus.

Alexander reassembles his army on the Indus delta and builds new fleet.

Summer   Krateros and part of army travel overland through the Bolān Pass to Alexandria-in-Arachosia.

Alexander crosses Gedrōsia (Baluchistan), which leads to a large loss of life.

Autumn   Departure of fleet under Nearkhos of Crete, which sails along northern coast of Arabian Sea.

Winter   Reunion of Alexander, Krateros and Nearkhos in Karmania (southern Iran).

Alexander continues on to Persia, while Nearkhos navigates the Persian Gulf.

324 BC

Spring   Alexander restores the tomb of Cyrus the Great at Pasargadai (Arr. *Anab.* 6.29.4–11).

'Sousa weddings', whereby Macedonian nobles take Persian brides and Alexander marries Stateira, eldest daughter of Dareios (Arr. *Anab.* 7.4.4–8) – within a year of Alexander's death, she is treacherously murdered by Rhoxane.

Summer Flight of Harpalos to Athens, taking 5,000 talents and 6,000 mercenaries (Diod. 17.108.6–8).

Mutiny of army at Opis in Babylonia over Alexander's 'orientalizing' (Arr. *Anab.* 7.6.1–2, cf. 12.2 where Alexander promises, after mutiny, children of mixed parentage will be brought up in Persia in Macedonian way, and he will take them to Macedonia and restore them to their fathers when they come of age).

'Reconciliation' banquet (Arr. *Anab.* 7.11.8–9).

Nikanor announces Exiles' Decree at Olympia (Diod. 18.8.2–7, cf. Harding 113, 122), Alexander's attempt to rid his empire of homeless mercenaries – Homer (*Il.* 24.513–14) says Zeus made men exiles ... did Alexander think only a god could undo the ugly problem of exiles' fate?

Autumn Death of Alexander's alter ego Hēphaistiōn at Ekbatana – 'Krateros loves the king; Hēphaistiōn loves me for myself'.

Alexander makes request to Greek *poleis* for deification and heroization of Hēphaistiōn.

Winter Alexander resides in Ekbatana.

Campaign against the still unsubdued Kossaians of the Zagros Mountains.

323 BC

Spring Alexander returns to Babylon – omens.

Preparation of fleet for expedition to Arabia and establishment of coastal settlements (Arr. *Anab.* 7.19.3–21.1).

Alexander chooses 30,000 Persian youths to learn Greek and receive Macedonian military training (Diod. 17.108.1–3, Plut. *Alex.* 47.3, cf. Arr. *Anab.* 7.23.3 who says Persians were to be enrolled in Macedonian phalanx).

Harpalos hunted down and executed in Crete.

Summer Death of Alexander in south palace at Babylon ('To the strongest ... he saw that there would be a great funeral contest over him': Arr. *Anab.* 7.26.3).

Perdikkas, *chiliarchēs* of *sōmatophylakes*, select bodyguard, assumes control of whole empire as regent (Dexippos *FGrHist* 100 F8 apud Harding 125A, Diod. 18.2.4, 3.1, cf. Just. 12.4.5).

Birth of Alexander IV, son of Alexander and Rhoxane.

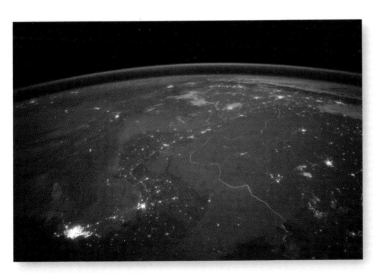

India–Pakistan border at night, 23 September 2015, looking north (NASA Photo ISS045-E-27869). Bottom left is the port city of Karachi, above and just to the right Hyderabad, centre right New Delhi, and top right the Himalayas. The dark green swathe is the Indus Valley. The serpentine 3,323km-border between Pakistan and India is illuminated by 150,000 flood lights installed by India that have a distinctive orange glow. Beyond the Jhelum is a large alluvial plain covering eastern Pakistan and north-western India. This is the Punjab Plain, which stretches all the way to the Ganges. Alexander probably followed the ancient road from Taxila to the Ganges. (ISS Expedition 45 crew/Wikimedia Commons/Public domain)

The long march: Alexander's route to the fringes of India

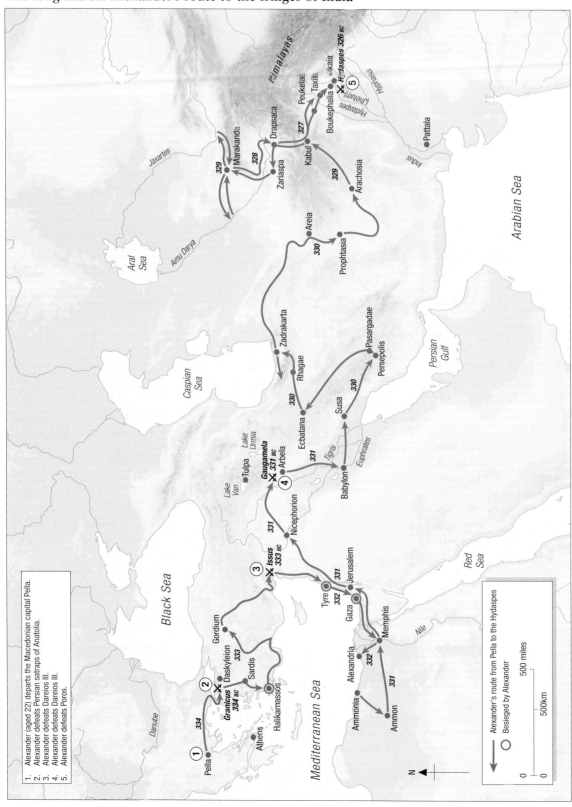

1. Alexander (aged 22) departs the Macedonian capital Pella.
2. Alexander defeats Persian satraps of Anatolia.
3. Alexander defeats Dareios III.
4. Alexander defeats Dareios III.
5. Alexander defeats Poros.

OPPOSING COMMANDERS

ALEXANDER

> The personality of the general is indispensable, he is the head, he is the all of an army ... It was not the Macedonian phalanx which penetrated to India, but Alexander.
>
> Napoleon Bonaparte, *Mémoires* (Paris 1823–25), Vol. II, p. 90

There are strong views on Alexander III of Macedon (b. 356 BC, r. 336–323 BC). There were back at the time and there still are, and the polarizing adoration and antagonism he inspires means most military historians (and fellow 'military geniuses', to use a term first coined by Clausewitz) have their own Alexander. Each of these men, and invariably they are men, has his own perspective, not to say prejudices, and truth, like beauty, lies in the eye of the beholder. There are three competing schools of thought when it comes to Alexander, but that does not distract from the fact that a view of him that is one-sided is bound to have missed the truth. That said, whether we choose to magnify his achievements and diminish his faults – for the revisionists this is akin to carefully pruning the branches of Alexander's biography – or adopt a revisionist view by de-heroizing Alexander – for the heroizers such dreary cynicism is like casting aspersions on a saint – or take up the middle ground amid the hero and the anti-hero, there are characteristics of this controversial figure that cannot be disputed.

For one, there is the extraordinary toughness of the man who sustained nine wounds, breaking an anklebone and receiving an arrow through his chest and the bolt of a catapult through his shoulder. He was twice struck on the head and neck by stones and once lost his sight from such a blow. Again, the bravery that bordered on sheer folly never failed him in the front line of battle, a position that few commanders since have considered proper. He set out to show himself a hero, and from the Granīkos to the Indus he left a trail of heroics that have never been surpassed and is perhaps too easily assumed among all his achievements. There are two ways to lead men: both to delegate all authority and limit the leader's burden; or to share every hardship and decision and be seen to take the toughest labour, prolonging it until every other man has finished. Alexander's method was the second – and perhaps the best example of this was his near-fatal heroics at Multan – and only those who have suffered the first can appreciate why his men truly adored him.

With his chameleon talents, Alexander was famously generous and he loved to reward the same show of spirit that he asked of himself. It is extraordinary how the Persian nobility learnt to admire him, but the double sympathy with the lives of Greece and Persia was perhaps Alexander's most unusual characteristic. Equally, he was impatient and often conceited. The same officers who worshipped him must often have found him impossible, and the murder of 'Black' Kleitos was an atrocious reminder of how royal petulance could become blind rage and provoke an unhinged act of cruelty. Kleitos had not only been a childhood friend but had saved his life at the Granīkos, too (Arr. *Anab*. 1.15.8, Diod. 17.20.6, Curt. 8.1.20), and the dark deed was done in the midst of a feast with his own hands. While he drank as he lived, sparing nothing, his mind was not slurred by excessive indulgence. He was not a man to be crossed or to be told what he could not do, and he always had firm views on exactly what he wanted. He seldom gave a second chance.

Marble statue head (Pélla, Archaeological Museum, inv. ΓΛ 15) of Alexander III of Macedon, turn of 3rd century BC copy of an earlier bronze statue – an official likeness possibly by Lysippos of Sikyon, Alexander's personal sculptor (Plut. *Alex*. 4.1, Plin. 7.125, 37.8) – found near Giannitsa, central Macedonia, northern Greece. Unlike his father Philip, who was a tough, bearded warrior, Alexander was rather more androgynous with his curling leonine hairstyle swept off the brow, smooth complexion and large, bulging eyes, as attested in our sources. Physically, however, Alexander had inherited all of his father's toughness against wounds and weather. This highly idealized likeness of Alexander shows the 'godlike' young monarch with long tousled hair and lips slightly parted, his head slightly tilted to the left, looking upward in what became known as the 'Lysippean gaze'. (© Nic Fields)

With an abrasive manner went self-discipline, speed and shrewd political sense. He had a bold grasp of political affairs, whether in his insistence that his expedition was the Greeks' reverse of Persian sacrilege, though most Greeks opposed it, or his brilliant realization that the ruling elite of his new empire should draw on Iranians and Macedonians together, while the army should stand open to any subject who could serve it. In the poetic words of Plutarch, Alexander mixed the lives and customs of men 'as in a loving cup' (*Mor*. 329e, cf. 330d, 342a–b). If this utopian vision is true (views differ), then the line between conquerors and conquered would have become confusingly blurred. In reality, of course, the more utopian the rhetoric that describes the destination, the less likely it is to be reached.

As a strategist Alexander took risks because he had to, but he always tried to cover himself (Gaugamela), and as a tactician he was unequalled (the Hydaspes). But self-confidence could override his latter quality, especially when Fortune unchained herself from his banner and turned her back on him, as she did during the march through Gedrōsia. Through Zeus-Ammon, Alexander believed the gods specially favoured him, through Homer, he had chosen the ideal of a hero, and for Homer's heroes there could be no turning back from the demands of honour. Each ideal, the divine and the heroic, was that of a romantic. And though a romantic should not be romanticized, Alexander was to become the stuff of legend even in his own short lifetime, while through the passage of the millennia his biography has gained many fantastical accretions.

In the spring of 334 BC Alexander chose to make the first landfall in Asia on the shoreline traditionally held to be the spot where the Greeks' black ships were beached throughout the ten harrowing years that they laid siege to

Macedonian horseman sitting on an animal skin saddle blanket and wielding a *xystón* while riding down a Persian, late 4th-century fresco (now lost) from a Macedonian tomb, Lefkadia (Mieza), northern Greece. This is a copy of a watercolour by K.F. Kinch (1889): the original fresco was destroyed when the tomb was damaged during construction of a nearby railway line. A long spear was introduced by Philip II as an item of equipment carried by Macedonian horsemen, a novelty that revolutionized horse-combat techniques and enable effective engagement against foot soldiers. It was under Philip and Alexander that the horseman really assumed a significant place in battle, rather than being relegated to skirmishing or scouting. The *xystón*, the shaft of which was possibly of European cornel wood and measured some 3.50–4.25m long, was far more effective for a charging horseman than the cornel-wood javelins (OP *aršti*) used by Persian horsemen (Arr. *Anab.* 1.15.5, cf. Xen. *Hell.* 3.4.14), or the cane javelins used by Indian horsemen. (Carole Raddato/Wikimedia Commons/ CC-BY-SA-2.0)

Troy. The 22-year-old king's mission was to take on the colossal power of the Persian empire with an army numbering 'not much above' 30,500 men (Arr. *Anab.* 1.11.3, cf. Plut. *Alex.* 15.1) and 'less than 60 talents in the treasury' (Arr. *Anab.* 7.9.6, cf. Plut. *Alex.* 15.2, who says 'no more than 70 talents').[1] We can easily envisage that such a piffling, impecunious and, as he probably believed, ephemeral invasion force should have excited the mirth of the Great King Dareios III, master of an empire that had stood for two centuries.

Alexander may have had a near-empty war chest, but he was young and warlike. Following the example of Homer's Protesilaos (*Il.* 2.701, Hdt. 9.116.3), the king immediately made his intentions clear by leaping ashore 'armed *cap-à-pie*' (Arr. *Anab.* 1.11.7) and symbolically casting a spear into the soil of Asia, a sign 'that he received Asia from the gods as a spear-won prize' (*Asían … doríktēton*: Diod. 17.17.2, cf. Just. 11.5.10). Next he performed a series of symbolic ritual acts intended to associate himself closely with the lofty warriors of the Trojan War, above all to his great forerunner, Achilles (Arr. *Anab.* 1.11.7–8, 12.1, Plut. *Alex.* 15.4–5, Diod. 17.17.3, Just. 11.5.12). Unsurprisingly, to quote J.R.R. Tolkien: 'History became legend. Legend became myth'.

Myths are powerful things. For one thing, they can create heroes and villains, martyrs and tyrants. There is the mosaic depicting the battle of Gaugamela (though art historians believe the battle to be Issos) from the Casa del Fauno at Pompeii, a Roman copy of a Greek painting done within living memory. This dazzling composition surely stands as the most powerful of all depictions of Alexander. With youthful acuity, Alexander strains forward, spurring his horse, eyes bulging and hair streaming, driven by his inner demon (when was he not?), his quasi-religious yearning, what the Greeks called *póthos*. To the passive viewer, the young king looks disarmingly berserker-like, a condition in which fear, the instinct for self-preservation, self-control and empathy all drop away and the man becomes

---

1   According to Polybios (12.19.1) and Plutarch (*Mor.* 327d–e), the contemporary historians gave the following figures (foot/ horse): Kallisthenēs 40,000/4,500; Ptolemaios 30,000/5,000; Aristoboulos 30,000/4,500; Anaximenes 43,000/5,500. It is evident that Arrianus followed Ptolemaios.

a killing machine. It comes as little surprise, therefore, to see fear and pain written all over the faces of his shattered Persian adversaries, including that of the Great King himself, Dareios III. As for Alexander's *póthos*, Arrianus hits this particular nail square on its head:

> For my part, I cannot ascertain with any accuracy what plans Alexander was pondering, nor is it my concern to guess, though I do not hesitate to assert that he would have planned nothing trivial or insignificant, nor would he have ceased striving no matter what he had already acquired, even if he had added Europe to Asia or the Britannic Isles to Europe. Instead, he would have sought beyond the known for something unknown, vying with himself in the absence of any other rival. (Arr. *Anab.* 7.1.4)

Immediately following this observation Arrianus expressly commends the Indian Gymnosophists for their view that 'each man can have only so much land as this on which we are standing' (ibid. 1.6), and Alexander, despite his praise for such a sentiment, acts in a way completely opposed to it. Arrianus refers to Alexander's *póthos* many times (ibid. 3.1.5, 5.25.2, 26.1, 7.1.1, 2.2), and it is clear for him his conquests are merely an expression of the conqueror's insatiable appetite for fame. Though plainly an avid admirer of the Macedonian conqueror, Arrianus identifies him as that individual hero who treads his own path of glory.

Two protagonists, the cosmic king and the alien aggressor, dominate the composition of the mosaic. On the left Alexander, with his head uncovered, remorselessly rushes forward on Boukephálas, 'Ox-head' (from βοῦς, 'ox', and κεφαλή, 'head') so called 'from the width of his head' (Strab. 15.1.29, cf. Arr. *Anab*. 5.19.5), the unruly horse that he famously tamed when he was a 12-year-old crown prince. Like a vengeful fury, the king wields a *xystón* with which he has just skewered a Persian soldier who had courageously rushed to the defence of Dareios. Hard on the heels of Alexander and snapped into combat-ready mode, are his helmeted companions. On the right of the composition, Dareios, in the yellow Persian tiara, stretches out his noble hand to his self-sacrificing saviour, while his charioteer whips the team to flee toward the right and out of the battle. Around him are his kinsmen – including his brother Oxyáthrēs (OP *Vakšuvarda*) – who mill in confusion around the royal four-horsed chariot, their faces filled with a mixture of dismay and determination. The lack of helmet coupled with the way he glowers directly at Dareios, makes this a dynamic portrait of Alexander. We are in no doubt who is the alpha male.

However we personally view Alexander, his conquest of the Persian empire was an extraordinary feat-of-arms – truly 'Homeric' in style and proportions. By 334 BC he had crossed over to Anatolia, the western half of the Persian empire, with Egypt being consolidated by 331 BC and the eastern half right up to the Indus just prior to his untimely death in 323 BC. Like Achilles, Homer's terror incarnate, he was doomed to an early death. Plutarch discloses that Alexander 'called the *Iliad* a viaticum of the military art … and always kept it lying with his dagger under his pillow, as Onēsikritos informs us' (*Alex.* 8.2). Such stories concerning Alexander are abundant, and whether they are real or apocryphal there are none that have not suffered some exaggeration. As Strabo was to point out, 'All those who wrote about Alexander preferred the marvellous to the true' (2.1.9). The choice blanches Alexander a bit of what makes him interesting, leaving him looking more fabulous than he really was.

In fable Alexander is flexible and regenerative, terrifying and charismatic, a cold-eyed malleable shapeshifter who is known as Iskandar or Sikandar (the spellings vary), and by the epithets 'the Great' (ὁ Μέγας), 'the Two-Horned One' (*Dhū al-Qarnayn*, Qur'ān 18:83–99), or one we do not hear often, 'the accursed' (*gizistag*, *Ardā Wirāz nāmag* 1.1–7). In Christian allegories Alexander appears as Christ and Poros as Satan, while the anonymous 14th-century Persian *Iskandar-Nāmeh* (*Book of Alexander*) has Alexander, now a Muslim prophet, decapitating Fur (i.e. Poros) for refusing to accept Islam. Romance has busied itself with his life and has converted Alexander into an anti-hero of his own tale.

Alexander is in a liminal state. He comes from the far north, from the fringes of the Greek world, and having made the apotheosis from warrior king to living legend he occupies a space somewhere between the human and the divine. This is a quality that his untimely death serves to increase. There is no doubting his talents, although it helped that he inherited a professional fighting machine and, of course, his career as a conqueror barely lasted 13 years. His achievements were not sustained by his successors, so we may wonder what his reputation might be like if he had lived as long as his father. So, where the real Alexander and fabled Alexander begin and end remains a question that does not really seem to have abated. Perhaps this is part of why he endures: he can mean whatever people want him to mean. Without a doubt, if Alexander had not existed, it would have been necessary to invent him. After all, Homer did that for Achilles.

Claudius Ptolemaios' *Decima Asiae Tabula: India intra Gangem* (Warszawa, Biblioteka Narodowa, inv. Rps BOZ 2/I-II), from the *Cosmographia Claudii Ptolomaei Alexandrini*, an ink and colour on parchment copy made in 1467 by the cartographer Nicolaus Germanus. Between the time of Herodotos (*fl.* 450 BC) and the time of Claudius Ptolemaios (*fl.* AD 150) the existence of India was known, but not its shape, and though they knew China (Gk. Σῆρες/*Sēres*) existed, no more than that was known. For the Greeks (and Macedonians), the known inhabited world ended in India, beyond which, according to Herodotos (3.98), there extended a sandy desert region, while the cartographer and mathematician Eratosthenes of Kyrēnē (apud Strab. 15.1.10) held that in Alexander's time the Indus was the boundary between the Persian empire and India. (Peacay/Wikimedia Commons/Public domain)

POROS

> The warrior's look is like a thunderous rain-cloud's, when, armed with mail, he seeks the lap of battle. May you be victorious with unwounded body: so let the strength of your mail protect you.
>
> *RV* 6.75.1

Πῶρος, Pōros (San. *Paurava*) is the name he goes by in the Greek sources, and what little is known about the Hindu raja (San. *rājan-*) has come down to us from these same writers. Unlike Alexander, Poros simply does not have as many (if any) storytellers on his side. Intriguingly, ancient Indian writers not only failed to mention Poros, but were practically silent about Alexander himself. Today it is quite a different matter, for Poros happens to be 'a great hero of the Panjab' who combined 'instinct with Herculean vigour and patriotic fervour' (Prakash 1967: 92). There are those who go further in believing that Poros and his Indian army had never been beaten by Alexander.

According to Michael Witzel (1997: 320 n. 320, 330–31 n. 326), Poros was the raja of the remains of the Pūru tribe of the *Ṛgveda* who existed as a marginal power between the rivers Hydaspes and Akesínes following their defeat at the semi-legendary battle of the Ten Kings. The *Mahābhārata* (2.27.15–17) refers to the city of the well-known ancient clan of the Pauravas, which was adjacent to the republic of Utsavasanketas and the territory of Kaṣmīra. A rich and populous kingdom, Strabo (15.1.29) alleges it contained almost 300 cities. Poros' neighbouring kingdom to the west, Taxila, was ruled by Āmbhi (Omphis to the Greeks), a member of his extended family, but their relationship was one of outright hostility: Poros was responsible for the assassination of the previous raja of Taxila, Ambhija, his maternal uncle and father of Āmbhi.

Poros is said to be 'five cubits tall' (Diod. 17.88.4, *Metz Epit.* 54), which either implies he was 2.3m if the Attic cubit (0.46m) is meant, or the more likely height of 1.78m if the shorter Macedonian cubit (0.355m) is meant (Tarn 1948: 2.170). Plutarch, on the other hand, has Poros stand at a more modest 'four cubits and a span' (*Alex.* 60.6), which translates as 2.07m or 1.6m. Arrianus agrees with Diodoros Siculus, adding the raja was 'of great personal beauty' (*Anab.* 5.19.1), while Curtius just says he had 'an unusually large physique' (8.13.7, cf. 14.13). He was, it might appear, a dazzling sovereign straight out of the heroic past.

In the Hindu epics and Buddhist canonical works, the raja habitually commands his army, and remains an active participant in battle. He invariably belongs to the *kṣatriya* or noble warrior class, and is duly trained in the art of handling an elephant, horse and chariot, and weapons such as the bow and the sword (*MN* II 69, 94). Courage, both constitutional and bodily, and leadership are the nuts and bolts of kingship, and its military role is indeed indivisible from the ruler's obligation to protect his people from threat of invasion without and civil strife within. This assumption is clearly stated by Kauṭilya, the Indian mastermind who wrote a definite treatise on statecraft: 'Where there is no raja wielding the sceptre of justice, the strong eat up the weak, as it is among fish' (*AS* 1.4, cf. *Mbh* 12.67, 122). So, the raja needs to be truly a ruler to his people as well as a warrior. Indeed, the *kṣatriyas* are described as the best of men by the Buddha (d. 486 BC), who places them even higher than the *brāhmaṇas* (*DN* I 99).

The Rāvī viewed from Nurpur fort, Kangra, Himachal Pradesh, India. One of the six rivers of the Indus System in the Punjab, the first phase of the battle of the Ten Kings was fought on the left bank of the Rāvī (then the Paruṣṇī). Alexander's army crossed the Rāvī – known as the Hydraōtēs to the Greeks – in the vicinity of Nainakot, the present border where north-western India was partitioned in August 1947. Having previously crossed the Akesínēs, Alexander attacked the autonomous Indians, who organized the first resistance at Sangala. The inhabitants of the neighbouring strongholds abandoned their homes and fled. Dividing his army into three columns, Alexander ruthlessly pursued the refugees; the sick and the slow were slaughtered attempting to ford the Hydraōtēs. (Harvinder Chandigarth/Wikimedia Commons/CC-BY-SA-4.0)

Poros would survive the slaughter of the Hydaspes. Having demonstrated he was the best of men, but losing the day all the same, Poros, according to Arrianus, was 'overcome by thirst' (*Anab*. 5.18.7). Diodoros Siculus (17.88.6), Curtius (8.14.38–40) and Plutarch (*Alex*. 60.7), on the other hand, have the raja tumbling to the ground half dead from multiple wounds, and being protected by his faithful elephant. Megasthenēs reports that Indian elephants, 'when their masters have sought refuge between their forelegs, have fought in their defence and saved their lives' (fr. 36 apud Strab. 15.1.42). Megasthenēs was the Greek envoy sent by Seleukos I Nikatōr to the court of his rival Chandragupta Maurya (r. *c*. 321–297 BC), the raja of Magadha (Strab. 2.1.9, 15.1.36), who came to power with the assistance of Kauṭilya.

The Buddha describes to his son 'a raja's bull elephant whose tusks are as long as a plough pole, massive, finely bred, whose home is the battlefield, and who, when going forth to battle, uses his forelegs, use his hind legs, uses the forepart of his body, uses the hind part of his body, uses his head, uses his ears, uses his tusks and uses his tail, protecting only his trunk' (*MN* I 414–15). In the *Mahābhārata* (2.49.7, 4.12.20, 30.26) 60-year-old elephants are always prized as being the most suitable age for battle service, and gifts of elephants at this age are looked on as particular generous. According to Curtius, the bull elephant Poros rode that fateful day 'towered above the other beasts' (8.13.7), and an Indian elephant can reach a shoulder height of 3.5m. Ironically enough, it would be elephants that were the cause of the noble raja's death.

The vicious encounter at the Hydaspes shows Poros as a fearless, noble and largely patriotic figure. In the words of Arrianus:

> [W]hen most of his infantry had perished, he did not emulate Dareios, the Great King, who retreated, the first of his men to flee. Instead, Poros stood his ground as long as any portion of the Indian force held firm.
>
> Arr. *Anab*. 5.18.4–5

Despite being scuttled that day, he duly impressed his opponent, for Arrianus reports that Alexander 'restored to Poros his sovereignty over his subjects, adding to his realm other territory of even greater extent' (*Anab*. 5.19.2, cf. Diod. 17.89.6, Curt. 8.14.45, Plut. *Alex*. 60.8). On his return westward, Alexander ratified Poros as the de facto ruler of these lands east of the Hydaspes and, unlike Āmbhi, was given no Macedonian satrap to watch over him and so was spared the imposition of a Macedonian garrison. Following the death of Perdikkas on the Nile – he was murdered in early 320 BC by his own officers, Peithōn and Seleukos – Antipatros was appointed *epimeletès*,

Bhir Mound, which represents the second urban centre of Taxila (Takshiçila). Dated 700–300 BC, this was a great seat of Vedic learning and famed for its physicians; the Buddha would come here for medical treatment. When Alexander arrived, raja Āmbhi liberally entertained the Macedonian king and, having previously offered his submission, provided troops for the coming fight against their common enemy Poros. The Bhir Mound coin hoard included Achaemenid coins of the 'archer king' type (Type II Sigloi) and coins of Alexander and his half-brother Philip III Arrhidaios (he would be liquidated in 317 BC by Olympias, Alexander's mother). After Alexander, Taxila would become one of the centres of Hellenic culture in India, and a nexus of East and West in art, architecture, language, poetry and philosophy. (Jona Lendering & Marco Prins/Wikimedia Commons/CC0 1.0 Universal)

The Kabul–Jalalabad Road. The difference in altitude between the two cities is some 1,200m and the road follows the Kabul River Gorge for 64km. The gorge, in places no more than a few hundred metres wide, is framed by a perpendicular wall of precipices that plummet 600m or so down to the river Kabul below. The road is part of the Grand Trunk Road, one of south Asia's oldest and longest routes, and is referred to in the *Mahābhārata* (12.207.43) as the *Uttarapatha*, the 'Northern road'. Because it enjoyed royal sanction, the Seleukid envoy Megasthenēs says Chandragupta Maurya had a whole army of officials overseeing the maintenance of what he refers to as the Royal Road. (Sven Dirks/Wikimedia Commons/CC-BY-SA-3.0)

protector, of the two hapless kings, the half-witted Arrhidaios (renamed Philip III) and the infant Alexander IV (in time, both would be murdered). According to Diodoros Siculus (18.39.6), Antipatros recognized Poros' authority over the lands he ruled. In 319 BC, the octogenarian Antipatros died. His death is said to have induced each general to work in his own interest (ibid. 50.1).

The miserable story of Poros' demise may be briefly told. In 317 BC, or shortly before, Eudēmos, commander of the Macedonian troops left in

Caparisoned Indian elephants at Sree Poornathrayesa temple festival, Thrippunithura, Kerala, India. At the Hydaspes, elephants presented Alexander's men with a new trial. Although Dareios had assembled 15 Indian elephants at Gaugamela, along with a contingent of Indian horsemen, they had not played any conspicuous part in the day's events there and ended up being captured (Arr. *Anab.* 3.8.6, 15.6). Alexander had close to 200 of them when he returned from India (Arr. *Ind.* 19.1), but he never relied upon elephants. It was left to Alexander's successors and their sons to incorporate these strange, imposing beasts into Hellenistic tactical thinking. Indeed, these pugnacious gentlemen became inordinately fond of war elephants, developing large herds of them as part of a pre-industrial arms race. They would use them in their fratricidal frays, so much so they became desirable adjuncts for every army in this period of continuous conflict, often on a massive and brutal scale. (Suresh Babu/Wikimedia Commons/CC-BY-SA-3.0)

Limestone stele (Paris, Guimet musee national des arts asiatiques) depicting women armed with small round shields and broad bladed swords. Their headgear is cloth, wound around their piled-up hair. Though this stele belongs to the Hindu kingdom of Vijayanagara (1336–1556), and sculptural cases of armed women are rare, their existence receives corroboration from Megasthenēs. He (*Indiká* fr. 27 apud Strab. 15.1.53–6) witnessed Chandragupta Maurya attended by armed women. The loyalty of female bodyguards was considered superior than their male counterparts, and Kauṭilya describes the need for strict security in the palace environs, where a polygamous monarch might be liquidated by one of his many wives or sons, and prescribes that he be guarded at night by his 'personal guard of female archers'. (© Esther Carré)

India, had Poros assassinated. By this act of treachery, Eudēmos secured 120 elephants (Diod. 19.14.8), which he subsequently brought to support Eumenēs of Kardia against Antigonos Monophthalmos, both former generals under Alexander.

Following his demise, one of Poros' sons,[2] Malayketu, ascended the throne with the backing of Eudēmos. His rapid rise to power precipitated an even more rapid fall. For the raja, if he is to be identified as Κητεὺς/*Kēteùs* mentioned by Diodoros Siculus (Prakash 1967: 91), was to be killed in action in late 317 BC at the battle of Paraitakēné (near Isfahan, Iran) 'after fighting brilliantly' (Diod. 19.33.1) at the head of his Indian troops. The kingmaker himself was executed by the would-be king Antigonos during the winter of 316 BC following his capture after the battle on the parched salt plain of Gabiene (ibid. 44.1). Back in India, meanwhile, the Macedonian conquests were rapidly conquered by Chandragupta Maurya (the Σανδρακόττος/ *Sandrakóttos* of the Greeks), who went on to swallow up the other Indian kingdoms to form an empire across much of northern India east of the Indus. But that is another story. Compared to Chandragupta Maurya, who as a youth 'saw Alexander himself' (Plut. *Alex.* 62.4), you do not hear much of Poros today, but trace elements of his existence survive when it comes to Alexander and his invasion of India.

---

2 Two of Poros' sons perished at the Hydaspes (Arr. *Anab.* 5.18.2), which implies the king had at least three sons, if not more. Just like Macedonian kings, Indian rajas were polygamous, and according to Diodoros Siculus, Malayketu 'had left two wives who had accompanied him in the army' (19.33.1).

OPPOSING FORCES

ALEXANDER'S ARMY

> The young Alexander conquered India. / He alone?
>
> Bertolt Brecht, *A Worker Reads History*, II.1–2

The army inherited by Alexander and the instrument of Persia's downfall, had already been forged by his father, Philip II of Macedon (r. 359–336 BC), into the most effective fighting machine of its day. It was to be Greece's ruin. As a hostage of Thebes during his informative years (probably 369–365 BC), Philip had been exposed to the innovations of the best hoplite *stratēgós* of the age, Epameinondas (d. 362 BC). Profiting from his lessons, Philip had grasped the Thebans' tactical manoeuvre of applying critical force at the enemy's strongest point by means of the oblique order of battle. This had resulted in the crushing defeat of the Spartans at Leuktra (371 BC), where Epameinondas had stacked the Theban phalanx 50-shields deep and rolled through the 12-deep Spartan phalanx. Consequently, the spell of Spartan invincibility was broken.

Philip's family also had close contacts with that other innovative *stratēgós*, Iphikrates of Athens (Aisch. 2.26–29). As a commander of mercenary peltasts (Gk. πελταστής/*peltastēs*), Iphikrates had taken care to combine in his men a high level of individual training and discipline – vital ingredients, if skirmishers are to be of service on the battlefield – with a strong *esprit de corps*. The most effective javelineers of their day, they could wear a hoplite phalanx down by missile fire if they kept their distance, as at Lechaion (390 BC) where Iphikrates almost annihilated an entire Spartan *móra* of 600 hoplites (Xen. *Hell.* 4.5.8–11).

Another of Philip's legacies was the expedition against Persia, a military contest of old and new would-be empires. In the spring of 336 BC, a few months before the day came when it was decided he should fall by the hand of an assassin, Philip had despatched a force of at least 10,000 men under two of his ablest *stratēgoi*, Parmeniōn and Attalos, to prepare a bridgehead for the military expedition he would lead against the Great King in the name of Greek revenge and his own self-aggrandisement (Polyain. 5.44.4, Diod. 19.91.2). Two years

Marble portrait bust (København, Ny Carlsberg Glyptotek, inv. 2466) of Philip II of Macedon, Roman copy of Greek original. After his charismatic, world-conquering son Alexander, Philip was the most famous and most distinguished king of Macedon, indeed, some commentators, ancient and modern, would regard him as the greater of the two monarchs. He was murdered in 336 BC at the relatively advanced age of 46. (Richard Mortel/Wikimedia Commons/CC-BY-SA-2.0)

Waxwork reconstructed head of Philip II modelled from the skull from Tomb II (the subject of some controversy), Vergina (Aigai, the capital of Macedon). The pioneering work of John Prag (archaeologist) and Richard Neave (medical artist), the great scar that was once his right eye is very stark. Philip's battle injuries are known. The list is given by Demosthenes (18.66-7): missing eye, broken collar bone, maimed arm and lame leg. The orator does not specify how the king lost the eye, or which eye, but Pompeius Trogus (Just. 7.6.14, cf. Diod. 16.34.5) says that during the siege of Methonē (354 BC), Philip had his right eye shot out by an arrow. According to the elder Pliny (7.37 §124) the arrow was extracted by the physician Kritoboulos of Keos, who was to do same for Alexander when he received an Indian arrow in the chest (Curt. 9.5.25-7, cf. Arr. *Anab.* 6.11.1). (Manolis Andronikos/ Wikimedia Commons/CC0 1.0 Universal)

later Alexander would do just that. In the fitting words of Frontinus, 'with 40,000 men who had already been trained by his father, Philip, Alexander of Macedon launched an attack on the world and vanquished enemy forces without number' (4.2.4). Like Hannibal Barca and Frederick the Great, Alexander owed his military know-how and his professional army to his father. He had not to invent; he had only to improve.

The architect

For contemporaries the success of Philip was due to the personal greatness of Philip himself. Theopompos of Chios, one of those contemporaries, said that 'Europe had never produced a man like Philip' (*FGrHist* 115 F27), and fittingly gave the title *Philippká* to his history of the period. In so doing he acknowledged the importance of the king's personality. This was a man, after all, who crucified his opponent, the Phokian Onamarchos, after he was killed in battle, and thought nothing of binding 3,000 of the latter's defeated mercenaries and throwing them alive into the sea 'as temple robbers' (Diod. 16.35.6). Theopompos recognized that Philip did what he did, and what his predecessors had been unable to do, because Philip was Philip and, unlike his son Alexander, he was a man whose genius lay in knowing when to ruthlessly exploit an advantage and when to prudently back off and bide his time.

Militarily the importance of Theopompos' aforementioned statement can hardly be exaggerated, primarily because Philip's innovations in strategy and tactics radically changed the existing practice of Greek warfare. In the 23 years of his reign (359–336 BC) Philip was to transform Macedon from a peripheral kingdom on the northern rim of the Greek world to being on the brink of world power. In a lengthy speech that Arrianus puts into his mouth, Alexander describes his father's transformation of the Macedonian people from 'vagabonds and paupers … into city-dwellers civilized by the gift of good laws and customs' (*Anab.* 7.9.2).

When Philip acceded to the throne at the age of 23, officially as the regent for his nephew Amyntas IV (d. 335 BC),[3] the very existence of Macedonia as an independent kingdom was hanging in the balance. Like all wise war leaders he moved very fast, first against his rival claimants. The outside world viewed Macedonia as a political jungle ruled by kings who broke their word and never died peacefully. On one account they were right, for Macedonian society was riven by intrigue and culled by frequent assassinations (Philip's father had come into power by assassination, while his two older brothers had met violent ends). Having rid himself of rivals, Philip then moved against his predatory neighbours. Like most other people, the Macedonians did not get to choose their neighbours. The immovable facts of geography were their fate: every neighbour was an enemy and the enemy's enemy was a friend. Until his accession, internal conflicts between rival nobles and meddling from

---

3 Amyntas was far too young to face the dangerous threat of the Illyrians and other enemies of Macedon (Just. 7.5.9–10); Alexander would have him eliminated on grounds of treason (Plut. *Mor.* 327c).

outsiders had kept Macedon from achieving its full potential. During his first five years Philip suppressed the former and developed the most efficient fighting force in the Greek world to coerce the latter. Innovation, training, and first-class leadership were the key.

Philip unashamedly ruled as an autocrat, maintaining his iron grip on the levers of power. Though Demosthenes, the king's sworn enemy and calumniator, labelled him as 'an unscrupulous and clever opportunist' (4.4), the Athenian orator also identified the bedrock upon which Philip built his power, namely 'his combined position in command of the army, state and exchequer' (4.5). Demosthenes was to return to this theme of absolutism after the Greeks' brutal loss to the Macedonians at Chairōneia in Boiotia (338 BC). The Athenian orator, who had neither forgiven nor forgotten Philip's crushing victory over the confederation forces of Thebes, Athens and Corinth, states the obvious: Philip owed his win that day to his 'absolute power over all his following, which in warfare is the greatest asset of all' (18.235). It could be said that the king was the state or, to borrow the words commonly attributed to Louis XIV, '*L'état, c'est moi*', who was saying, in effect, my will is the law. For the French king, as Philip did long before him, united in his own person a near-monopoly of executive powers and privileges in the religious, judicial, diplomatic, political and military spheres.

Yet to Philip the state was a mere ancillary to the army, and therefore was organized on the sole principle of providing manpower, labour and capital to ensure the formidable Macedonian army would be fuelled for further aggrandisement. Philip's territorial ambitions had nothing to do with a few hectares outside the *polis*, but rather encompassed a broader vision of mines, harbours, and tribute-paying communities. Thus, for instance, the physical takeover of the Thracian gold mines of Mount Pangaîos, annexed – along with the ill-fated *polis* of Amphipolis – in 357 BC, gave him 'a revenue of more than 1,000 talents' (Diod. 16.8.7, cf. Dem. 23.111, Harding 70). This allowed him to keep his *paid* army on constant operations, as well as enabled him to swell its ranks with highly paid Greek mercenaries. Indeed, Philip's financial power was comparatively unmatched, except by the Great King of

Persia, and it gave him invaluable advantages. And so it was this wealth that allowed Philip the wherewithal to hire mercenaries and to bribe foreign politicians. Demosthenes (18.246–47) himself reckoned the king could bribe into bondage anyone in Greece. Philip himself once said that few armies were as powerful as a single donkey heavily laden with sacks of gold, and opined he could take any city by driving into it a donkey decked so. For Philip, the strategy of war was designed predominately as a device of ambitious state policy, and turning old enemies into new friends, or at least allies, was one of his many ploys.

Boot camp

'Privitations, poverty, misery – these are the school for good soldiers', so wrote the young Napoleon Bonaparte.[4] This of course was no new regime. So as to strengthen their backs and harden their feet, Philip fully expected his soldiers to carry their full panoply as well as provisions on the march. In the words of Polyainos:

> Philip accustomed the Macedonians to constant exercise before actual warfare by making them march often 300 *stadia* (*c.* 60km), bearing their arms and carrying besides their helmets, shields, greaves, spears [*sarissae*?] and their provisions, as well as utensils for daily use. (Polyain. 4.2.10)

So, shunning the practices of contemporary Greek and Persian armies, Philip also forbade the use of wagons and carts, and limited attendants to one for every ten foot soldiers and one for every horseman to carry hand mills for grinding grain and other gear such as tents and ropes (Frontin. 4.1.6). Philip also forbade women to tag along with the army when it went to war (Athēn. 13.557b), a doctrine that would be maintained by Alexander (Arr. *Anab.* 1.24.1).

Philip probably instituted this reorganization of the army in response to his campaigns in the mountainous regions of Thrace, Paionia, and Illyria. Here the use of wagons and carts would be impractical if not impossible over mountain paths, and where large numbers of camp followers would not only slow the army down but also make it especially vulnerable on the march. The consequence of these logistical reforms was to make the Macedonian army faster and lighter, and thus more mobile than any other contemporary organized army. The essence of speed was important in Macedonian strategy and Demosthenes certainly highlights Philip's capacity to make 'sudden raids' (4.17, cf. 9.49–51). Philip had created an army much lighter in terms of what it took with it on campaign.

---

4   Napoleon Bonaparte, 'Campaignes d'Italie (1796–1797)', *Correspondance*, vol. 29, p. 84.

Alexander, unsurprisingly, retained the streamlined logistical system imposed by his father (Plut. *Alex.* 60.4, Curt. 4.9.17, 20, 7.5.16, 8.2.5, 15, 9.10.15, Arr. *Anab.* 3.21.3, 7, Diod. 17.55.4 [arms and armour], Curt. 8.4.20, Arr. *Anab.* 3.2.1, 3 [rations], Curt. 4.9.19–21 [backpacks], Arr. *Anab.* 3.2.1, 6.6.2 [utensils], ibid. 1.24.1 [women]). As Frontinus rightly points out:

> Alexander of Macedon conquered the world, in the face of innumerable forces of enemies, by means of 40,000 men long accustomed to discipline under his father Philip. (Frontin. 4.2.4)

Still, even Alexander could not alter the habitual behaviour of his fighting men, and later he relaxed the strictures regarding camp followers, permitting them to marry and maintain women (Just. 12.4.2). This was partly to dull their longing for their homeland but also to produce a new generation of young men who could be recruited in their turn. Soon enough, the army was followed by a host of women, wains, soothsayers, sutlers and servants that doubled its size, not to mention the baggage train heaving with Indian booty. But this change led to a number of tragedies, such as many non-combatants dying of thirst and hunger during the unfortunate and unnecessary crossing of the Gedrosian desert.

Macedonian phalanx

As Macedonia was a poor country on the northern rim of the Greek world, the Macedonian phalanx was composed of peasant levies – all healthy male subjects of the king were liable for service – who could ill afford the panoply of a Greek hoplite. Consequently, they were issued, at state expense, with the *sarissa* ('long-spear') and light body armour. As the new weapon required both hands for adequate control and handling, a bronze-faced, button-

Sarissa heads (Chairōneia, Archaeological Museum) discovered in the mass grave of the Macedonians who fell at Chairōneia (338 BC). The best-preserved head, though missing some of its point and socket, still has a total length of 38cm; its size shows that it cannot have come from anything but a *sarissa* (Sotiriades 1903: 309 and pl. 41, no. 7). The heart of Macedonian warfare was the phalanx at the centre of the battle line, like a hedgehog, or sectioned like a series of hedgehogs, 16- or sometimes 32-ranks deep. Whereas the *hetaîroi* were recruited from the scions of the aristocratic families of the kingdom's diverse regions, the *pezhétairoi* were drawn from the Macedonian peasantry and equipped by the state. They underwent a rigid training régime to ensure they were proficient at handling the *sarissa*. (Jona Lendering/Livius. org/CC0 1.0 Universal)

shaped shield, about eight palms (c. 60cm) in diameter, was hung from the neck by means of a shoulder strap and manoeuvred with the forearm as required (Polyain. 4.2.10, Askl. 5.1, Polyb. 18.29.2). It is assumed the shield was conveniently slung on the back when not in use.

Before the reign of Philip the kingdom's infantry was a less evolved species of soldiery (Thuc. 4.124.1, cf. 2.100.5, an illuminating passage). Still, the mobilization of the peasantry as a political tool, as well as a military force, may pre-date Philip if the testimony of Anaximenes is correct. He says (*FGrHist* 72 F4) a certain Alexander, probably Philip's eldest brother Alexander II, created and organized Macedon's first heavily armed infantry, and awarded them the honorific title of 'foot-companions' (Gk. πεζέταιροι/ *pezhétairoi*) to enhance their prestige. But Alexander II only reigned for a single year (369–368 BC) – a rival assassinated him – which seems too short for significant military reorganization. The first mention of the *pezhétairoi* in a historical context is in 349 BC, as part of the army of Philip fighting around Olynthos and as having 'the reputation of being remarkably well trained in military matters' (Dem. 2.17).

It could be argued that the introduction of the ten to 12 cubit- (4.6–5.5m; Askl. 5.1, Theophr. 3.12.2, cf. Polyb. 18.28.2 where he says 'the length of the *sarissae* is 16 cubits [7.3m] according to the original design') long *sarissa* as the principal offensive infantry weapon was actually Philip's innovation. Of course, we would have to posit that the later translation of Anaximenes' text had been corrupted from the original 'Philip father of Alexander' to just 'Alexander'. It has been argued (Markle 1977) that the phalangite was not armed with the *sarissa* until sometime after the battle of Chaironeia (338 BC). Conversely, that is was Philip's innovation is certainly implied by Diodoros Siculus:

> [Philip] built up their morale, and, having improved the organization of his forces and equipped the men suitably with weapons of war, he held constant manoeuvres of the men under arms and competitive drills. Indeed he devised the compact order and the equipment of the phalanx, imitating the close-order fighting with overlapping shields of the warriors at Troy [i.e. *Il*. 13.131–34, cf. Polyb. 18.29.6, Curt. 3.2.13], and was the first to organize the Macedonian phalanx. (Diod. 16.3.1–2)

Philip's first major battle was against the Illyrians near Lake Lychnitis early in the campaigning season of 358 BC. Diodoros Siculus, drawing upon the contemporary Theopompos (*FGrHist* 115 F348), says that Philip led the right wing of his army, 'which consisted of the flower of the Macedonians' (16.4.5). It is assumed that Diodoros Siculus is referring here to the *pezhétairoi*, Philip having:

> [O]rdered his companion cavalry (*hetaîroi*) to ride past the barbarians and attack them on the flank, while he himself fell on the enemy in a frontal assault. (Diod. 16.4.5)

So, by leading them in person, Philip gave the newly established Macedonian phalanx a psychological boost. The Illyrians, by the way, attempted to form a square but were annihilated before completing the manoeuvre, leaving more than 7,000 dead on the field (ibid. 6).

Pílos helmet (Athens, National Archaeology Museum), a simple bronze conical type commonly worn by Alexander's *pezhétairoi.* This style of helmet derives from a felt conical cap actually called the *pílos,* which was possibly initially worn as a protection underneath close helmets and later translated into bronze. The *pílos* helmet was light and provided all-round vision, and seems to have been adopted by the Spartans first. The helmet terminates in a discernable point, very much like a sugarloaf, and has a narrow rim that does not stick out at all but follows the line of the crown, hanging almost vertically from the body of the helmet. (Dorieo/Wikimedia Commons/ CC-BY-SA-4.0)

Regrettably, the archaeological record does not help as the earliest *sarissa* heads to date are those that were found at the battle site of Chairōneia, close to the end of Philip's reign (Sotiriades 1903). When Diodoros Siculus says Philip 'yielded the dead for burial, gave sacrifices to the gods of victory' (16.86.6), he infers a single burial place. The *sarissa* heads themselves were discovered near the river Kephissos in the group burial mound, the *polyándrion* (Plut. *Alex.* 9.2), of the Macedonian dead from the battle. They are now on display in the local Chairōneia museum. Despite the lack of firm evidence, however, the organization of the deadly Macedonian phalanx, which counts as the greatest single tactical innovation of what can be regarded as a new model Macedonian army, should be attributed to Philip and not his eldest brother Alexander II.

Perceived wisdom has it that the *sarissa* was made of a long shaft of hard elastic wood called European cornel (Gk. κράνεια/*kráneia*, L. *Cornus mas*). In truth, Theophrastos does not actually make it clear this was the type of wood used. What he actually says is that the 'height of the 'male' [cornel] tree is at most 12 cubits, the length of the longest Macedonian *sarissa*' (3.12.2), adding that the trunk does *not* grow straight. If indeed cornel was used, and it is no means certain, then this may be one of the reasons why the shaft was of a two-piece construction fitted together by an iron or a bronze coupling sleeve. Equipped with an iron leaf-shaped blade and bronze butt-spike – both about 50cm in length – and weighing just over 4kg (Connolly 2000: 105–8, cf. Markle 1977: 324), a 12-cubit *sarissa* was held with a two-handed grip 1.8m from the butt.

OPPOSITE

Companion horseman depicted in high relief on the massive carved 'Alexander Sarcophagus' (İstanbul, Arkeoloji Müzeleri, invs. 72–74) found at the necropolis of Sidon, constructed of Pentelic marble and dated late 4th century BC. Following Issos (333 BC) Alexander, having deposed the pro-Persian Straton II of Sidon, entrusted his greatest intimate Hēphaistiōn to find a successor. He appointed Abdalonymos, a distant relative of Straton now serving as a gardener, and it seems probable that he commissioned the sarcophagus soon after his accession. The horseman perhaps represents Hēphaistiōn, who was to Alexander what Patroklos was to Achilles, and the carving is part of the depiction of Alexander fighting the Persians at Issos. Traces of the original paint can be seen, though the bronze attachments representing weaponry have long gone. (© Nic Fields)

If handled with strength and discipline, its advantage over the shorter weapon carried by a Greek hoplite – a long thrusting spear (Gk. δόρυ/*dóru*) some 2.1–3.0m in length – is obvious. For the *sarissa* extended some 3.6m in front of the phalangite, thus giving him an advantage in reach of over 2.4m more than the hoplite. In addition, instead of the first two ranks, five ranks were now thrusting with their weapons, giving 40 per cent more spearheads in the killing zone; the rest kept their weapons vertical and used their body weight to increase the momentum of the front line (Polyb. 18.29.2–30.4, Ael. 14.6, Arr. *Takt.* 12.11). The hedgehog of their serried *sarissae* provided an unusual degree of offensive might, as well as defensive protection for the lightly armoured initial ranks. The butt-spike could be anchored in the ground to blunt charges by the enemy, and being of bronze meant it did not rust. An awkward weapon, the butt-spike also served to balance out the *sarissa*, making it easier to wield, and could be used as a back-up if the weapon snapped during the push and shove of combat.

Under Philip the usual depth of the phalanx may have been ten ranks, as a file in Alexander's army was called a decade (Gk. δεκάς/*dekás*). At some stage Alexander adopted the Greek system of using multiples of eight. The philosopher Kallisthenēs, a relative of Alexander's one-time teacher Aristotle who accompanied the king's expedition as official historian but was to perish at Alexander's hands in 327 BC, is quoted by Polybios as claiming that Alexander drew up his phalanx at Issos (333 BC) with 'a depth of 32 ranks, which he then dropped to 16 and then, finally, as it approached the enemy, eight' (12.19.5). As a former soldier, Polybios (12.19.6) is rather sceptical that an eight-deep phalanx could have been deployed in the available space, but he does not query the three possibilities. However, it is not until Alexander was drafting Persians into his depleted Macedonian army (323 BC), that we are given the first glimpse of the structure of the new-style phalanx.

Arrianus (*Anab.* 7.23.3) has each *dekás* consisting of 16 men. This composite Macedonian/Persian file was commanded by a *dekádarchos* who served in the front rank. Behind him came first a man on double pay (Gk. διμοιρίτης/*dimoirítēs*) and then a 'ten-stater' man, who was receiving less than double pay but more than the common pay of the rank and file. Behind the three Macedonians came the 12 Persians and bringing up the rear another 'ten-stater' man. Strangely enough, Arrianus says these Persian phalangites 'carried bows or thronged javelins' (ibid. 4). Diodoros Siculus, on the other hand, tells us that they 'were splendidly equipped with the full Macedonian armament' (17.108.2), which certainly seems more logical vis-à-vis maintaining the tactical effectiveness of the phalanx.

The phalanx itself was divided into *taxeis*, each *taxis* with the paper strength of 1,500 men and levied on a territorial basis. In Alexander's day there were 12 *taxeis*, six remaining in Macedonia and six taken on the invasion of Persia (Diod. 17.17.3, 5). They appear to have been functionally known by the name of their *taxiárchēs* (Arr. *Anab.* 3.11.9). At the Hydaspes, however, there would be seven *taxeis* (ibid. 5.11.3 with 12.1–2, following Tarn 1948: 2.191), which was probably the result of the reinforcements sent to Alexander in Sousa (Arr. *Anab.* 3.16.11). The seven *taxiárchoi* were the one-eyed Antigenes, Polyperkhon (Perdikkas' brother), Meleagros, Alketas (Amyntas' brother), Attalos (son of Andromenes), Gorgias, and 'White' Kleitos (Arr. *Anab.* 5.11.3, 12.1, 2, 16.3).

Still, to be tactically successful, the Macedonian phalanx needed a rank-and-file that was tough, disciplined and well trained. These requirements certainly tie in with Philip's regime to toughen up his soldiers by forced marches under arms and loaded down with rations and equipment (Diod. 16.3.1, Polyain. 4.2.1, 2, 10, 15, Frontin. 4.1.6). Unlike the 'muscle-bound' phalanx the Romans would meet a century or so hence, that of Alexander was capable of rapid movement and was highly manoeuvrable. The use of tightly packed spearmen in the phalanx may have been a Greek development, but it reached its peak of efficiency and prowess in the Macedonian armies commanded by Philip and Alexander. Immensely trained, immensely bold, immensely proud of its traditions, on the red field of battle Alexander's phalanx would be a terror to behold.

Hetaîroi

This phalanx of grim, professional *pezhétairoi* fought in concert with the 'companion cavalry' (Gk. ἑταῖροι/*hetaîroi*), an elite body of aristocratic horsemen riding strong mounts, and heavily armoured in Boiotian helmet, a very popular cavalry type as it 'affords the best protection … without obstructing the sight' (Xen. *PH* 12.3), bronze plate cuirass or linen corselet with *pteruges*, and possibly strap-on greaves. These horsemen were not showy youths like those of Athens, but independent tough scions of the Macedonian nobility whose desire was to charge into infantry not around them. They were armed with a spear (Gk. ξυστόν/*xystón*) some 3.50–4.25m in length, again possibly made from strong European cornel wood and with a butt-spike, and carried a single-edged slashing weapon heavier towards its point and with a curved blade (Gk. κόπις/*kópis*), the hilt of which was shaped like the head of a beast or bird of prey. Artistic evidence reveals that the *kópis* was characteristically used in an overarm stroke brought down from above the head or shoulder (see image on page 35). It is noteworthy that one of the Hippokratic medical treatises records that wounds delivered from above, as would be the case of those most commonly inflicted from horseback upon foot soldiers, are worse than ones inflicted from the same level (*DCV* 11).

The *hetaîroi* always took their place on the right, tactically the more aggressive wing under Alexander's direct command. The usual tactical deployment was the wedge formation (Ael. 18.4, Askl. 7.3) – like a 'flight of cranes' (Ael. 18.6) – ideally suited to punch holes in the enemy's battle line and widen it (Arr. *Takt.* 16.6–7). Their disciplined manoeuvring at speed added to their formidable power. In this sense, under the generalship of Philip and Alexander, cavalry assumed a significant place in combat, rather than being employed as mounted skirmishers as was the case with contemporary Greek or Persian horsemen.

The *hetaîroi* Theopompos (*FGrHist* 115 FF224–5, cf. Diod. 17.17.4) describes are probably those of the early 340s BC as the number of horsemen he gives, namely 800 as opposed to the 1,800 of Alexander's day (Diod. 17.17.4, cf. Arr. *Anab.* 6.14.4), fits with the number of *hetaîroi* that we would expect to find at this date. Yet the author's description here unmistakably exaggerates the wealth of the *hetaîroi* in order to blacken Philip's reputation. Demosthenes, as might be expected, also set out to disparage Philip's *hetaîroi*, but even he had to admit that they had a reputation as 'admirable soldiers, well grounded in the science of war' (2.17, cf. 11.10). Of particular interest is an extant fragment of Mnesimakhos' satire *Philippos*, produced shortly after 346 BC, in which one of them speaks for himself:

Know you now with what men you must fight?
With us, who sup upon well-sharpened swords,
And swallow lighted firebrands for dainties:
And then, for our dessert, our slaves bring in,
After the first course, Cretan bows and arrows;
And instead of vetches, broken heads of spears,
And fragments of well-battered shields and breastplates;
And at our feet lie slings, and stones, and bows,
And on our heads are wreaths of catapults.
(Mnesimakhos apud Athēn. 10.421b)

The verse of Mnesimakhos makes it sound more like one of Baron von Münchausen's boozy tall stories. Allowing for obvious immoderate embroidery, however, this fine piece of self-praise has a definite ring of truth about it.

Grave stele (Thebes, Archaeological Museum) bearing a low relief carving of a companion horseman. He wears a Boiotian helmet, bronze muscular corselet and bears a *xystón*. The cloak is a *chlamýs* (χλαμύς), typical Greek military attire in the form of a seamless rectangle of woollen material roughly the dimension of a blanket, commonly bordered. It was typically pinned with a *fibula*, as shown here, at the right shoulder. A creation of Philip II, who employed the *hetaîroi* as the hammer to the anvil of the *pezhétairoi*, it was this mounted assault force that decided all of Alexander's major pitched battles. (© Nic Fields)

The tactical unit of Alexander's cavalry was what we would call a squadron (Gk. ἴλη/*ílē*). Alexander himself led one *ílē* of *hetaîroi*, the *ílē basilikē*, which would have acted as his bodyguard when he fought on horseback. It was the first and largest of eight territorial *ílai* that accompanied him on his expedition to Asia (Arr. *Anab.* 3.11.8). Commanded by an *ilarchēs*, each *ílē* varied between 180 and 225 men, though the *ílē basilikē* comprised 300 men. These eight *ílai* of *hetaîroi* were supplemented by four *ílai* of *pródromoi* ('fore-runners') or *sarissophoroi* ('sarissa-bearers'), Macedonian horsemen armed with a shorter version of the *sarissa* (though still requiring both hands to wield it) and acting as scouts, and one *ílē* of Paionians.

Following the execution of Philotas, son of Parmeniōn, in the autumn of 330 BC, Alexander divided the *hetaîroi* between two *hipparchoi*, Hēphaistiōn and 'Black' Kleitos, so as to avoid the concentration of too much power in the hands of a single individual (Arr. *Anab.* 3.27.4, cf. 29.7). After Kleitos' murder he went further in the same direction; from 327 BC there were eight *hipparchoi* (ibid. 4.22.7, 23.1, 24.1, 6.16.1, cf. 7.6.4). Pompeius Trogus composes a neat formula to sum up the difference between Philip and Alexander: 'The one wished to reign with his friends, the other reigned over them' (Just. 9.6.17).

Hypaspistai

Another Macedonian speciality was the *hypaspistai*, 'shield-bearers', a name that is something of a puzzle. Though some scholars believe the *hypaspistai* were already an existing unit of Philip's army, they are first attested in an Attic inscription *(IG 2² 1.329.9–10)* dated to 336/335 BC in which we learn that the rate of pay of Alexander's *hypaspistai* was a *drachma* per day.

Whether or not they existed previously, in Alexander's army the *hypaspistai* were elite foot soldiers specially selected for their skill and physique, perhaps more lightly armed than the phalangites but more heavily than the peltasts. It is known they formed a unit distinct from the phalanx, deploying immediately on the right of the phalanx in the battle line to act as a link between it and the *hetaîroi*. But again, scholarly opinions differ as to their equipment, some even going so far to suggest they carried the *aspís* and *dóru* of the Greek hoplite (e.g. Markle 1977: 329–30).

At some point, probably in India (Arr. *Anab.* 7.11.3, Just. 12.7.5), the *hypaspistai* decorated their shields with silver and changed their name to *argyaspides*, 'Silver-shields'. During the early tumultuous wars of the Diadochoi (323–316 BC) they were best known, though perhaps unfairly, for their cold-hearted betrayal of Eumenēs of Kardia, an inveterate loyalist to the Argead dynasty. The *hypaspistai*, some 3,000 in number, were organized into *khiliarkhies* 1,000-strong under the command of a *khiliarkhēs* (Arr. *Anab.* 4.30.5). The first of the *khiliarkhía*, know as the *agēma*, acted as the king's bodyguard when he fought on foot. The Greek term *agēma* meant 'that which is led', but amongst the Macedonians the significance was rather 'that which leads'. At the Hydaspes the *hypaspistai* would be under the command of Seleukos (ibid. 5.13.4, cf. 16.3), who became one of the greatest of those who followed Alexander (ibid. 7.22.5).

Allies and auxiliaries

The indispensable complement of the Macedonian army comprised the lightly armed troops. Some of these troops may have come from Macedonia proper, but there is little explicit evidence. Arrianus, for instance, occasionally mentions *taxeis* of lightly armed troops, but he rarely gives an indication of their provenance and never designates any of them as Macedonian. On the other hand he does include Thracians and Agrianians among the *taxeis* of javelineers.

The most important of Alexander's lightly armed troops were 'the thousand Agrianoi' (Arr. *Anab.* 4.25.6), a body of crack javelineers from

Known as the Coif Chişinău (Chişinău, Muzeului Naţional de Arheologi şi Istorie a Moldovei), a 4th-century BC Phrygian helmet. Part of the Olăneşti treasure discovered in 1960, it is one of six helmets (along with five greaves and a bronze oil lamp bearing an inscription in ancient Greek), which apparently belonged to a Macedonian army under the command of Zopyrion – left as governor of Thrace by Alexander – who led an invasion of Scythian lands and perished with his troops in the winter of 331 BC (Curt. 10.1.44, cf. Just. 12.2.15). Also known as the Thracian helmet, the Phrygian form was the most common infantry type in use during the 4th century BC, having replaced the earlier Corinthian type. (CristianChirita/Wikimedia Commons/CC-BY-SA-3.0)

the upper valley of the Strymón (Struma) River. Herodotos and Appianus (*Illyrike* 14) describe them as a tribe of Paionia, but Theopompos says they were Thracians. Paionians or Thracians, these javelineers are attested more than 27 times in Arrianus alone, and were employed on almost every occasion that called for rapid movement on difficult terrain. In formal battle (Issos, Gaugamela) they were commanded by a Macedonian officer, Attalos (Arr. *Anab*. 2.9.2, 3.12.2, 21.8), and were posted to the right of the *hetaĩroi*, a position of considerable honour. Their usual associates were the Cretan archers (each unit appears only once on its own).

Once again there may have been a body of Macedonian archers but its numbers were small. Otherwise the archers largely comprised Cretans. The Greeks themselves used a self-bow made of a single flexible wooden staff. Cretan archers, on the other hand, who were specialists and thus often hired as mercenaries, used the composite recurve bow. This particular type of bow consisted of a wooden core on to which was laminated sinew (back) and horn (belly). The elasticity of the sinew meant that when the bow was drawn it stretched and was put under tension. By contrast, the strips of horn were compressed. By exploiting their mechanical properties, both materials thus reacted to propel the bowstring. This type of bow was very difficult to string and required the use of both legs and arms. There are occasional references to Cretans, who specialized in ruses and ambushes, with small round shields. The shields suggest these men were also armed with swords and thus prepared to fight hand-to-hand. Alexander certainly sometimes used his Cretans in circumstances in which they would have found such equipment useful.

The other major lightly armed group was the 7,000-strong contingent of Thracians, Triballians and Illyrians. Of these the Thracian javelineers or peltasts, under the Odrysian prince Sitalces, were prominent, performing the same function on the left of the skirmish line as the Agrianoi on the right. The peltast was named after the light shield (Gk. πέλτη/*péltē*) he carried. According to Aristotle (fr. 498 Rose) it was of wicker construction, rimless and covered with goat or sheepskin. Although he implies that the shield was round, pottery iconography invariable depicts it as crescent shaped, a segment being cut out of the top edge. The Thracian peltast, as earlier immortalized by Herodotos (7.75) and Xenophon (*Anab.* 7.4.4), wore the traditional costume of his cold country: brightly coloured, geometric-patterned heavy cloak (*zeíra*), high fawn-skin boots (*embádes*) and fox-scalp cap with earflaps. As for the other lightly armed troops serving in Alexander's army, he wore no armour and relied on his speed to get him out of trouble. His weapons were a pair of javelins and a short sword or dagger. Fighting in a loose-order formation, his tactic was to run in, launch javelins and then sensibly run away before the enemy could come to grips with him.

Of the allied contingents the most important by far were the Thessalian horsemen, considered the best in Greece and probably equal in number to the *hetaîroi* (Diod. 17.17.4), and more or less equal in calibre. Philip had been elected *tagos* of Thessaly, a title which transferred to Alexander. The Thessalians were a people essential for Alexander's army and control of southern Greece. Thessalians formed part of the defensive left wing of Alexander's army, which was regularly commanded by Parmeniōn, until they mustered out and returned home after the conquest of Persia. Like the *hetaîroi* they were divided into regionally based *ilai*, of which the Pharsalian horsemen were 'the finest and most numerous' (Arr. *Anab.* 3.11.10), and they performed much the same functions as the *hetaîroi* themselves. Weapons seem to have been the standard Greek choice of javelins and spears. Body armour, if worn, was a metal plated cuirass or simple material corselet with

Attic Red-Figure *pelíkē* (London, British Museum, inv. 1846, 0925.10) in the manner of the Kleophon Painter and dated *c.* 430 BC. Side A depicts a Thracian warrior standing before Orpheus, king of the Thracian tribe of Kikones and famous bard of Greek legend, playing his lyre. The warrior wears the distinctive outfit of Thrace; the fox-scalp cap with ear flaps, known as an *alōpekís*, and the long cloak (decorated with dotted strips and battlements) known as a *zeíra*. He is armed with two javelins. Thracians tended to shun armour so as to fight as light as possible. (ArchaiOptix/ Wikimedia Commons/ CC-BY-SA-4.0)

pteruges and that very popular equestrian headpiece, the Boiotian helmet. A high boot of an originally Thracian style, recommended by Xenophon (*PH* 12.10), was now popular with Greek horsemen. At this date Greek (or Macedonian) horsemen did not carry shields.

The rest of the allied horsemen, predominantly from central Greece and the Peloponnese, were much less important and effective, fewer in number and less prominent in action. Like the Thessalians they were divided into *ilai* under the command of a Macedonian officer. The Thracian cavalry comes in the same category, being placed alongside the Greek horsemen at the Granīkos (334 BC) and Gaugamela (331 BC), but the other cavalry body from the north, the Paionians, had a more distinguished career. They are associated with the *pródromoi* and were in the vanguard of fighting at the Granīkos and Gaugamela, but their numbers must have been small as with the Thracians they only amounted to 900 horsemen.

Both Macedonians and Persians made extensive use of Greek mercenaries, especially hoplites. But the numbers of Greeks in Persian service were substantially larger: 20,000 are attested at the Granīkos and 30,000 at Issos (Arr. *Anab.* 1.14.4, 2.8.6), whereas Alexander led only 5,000 hoplite mercenaries to Asia (Diod. 17.17.3, cf. Arr. *Anab.* 1.18.1 and 5). This was

Thessalian horseman from the 'Alexander Sarcophagus' (İstanbul, Arkeoloji Müzeleri, invs. 72–74). The horseman wears a Boiotian helmet, a *linothōrax* with tasselled *pteruges*, and a *chlamýs* pinned with a *fibula* at the right shoulder. He is armed with a *xíphos* (ξίφος), a straight, double-edged sword with a leaf-shaped blade and spindle-shaped hilt, and was probably originally depicted with a *xystón* (originally rendered as a bronze attachment, now missing). Thessalian horsemen were the second most important cavalry in Alexander's army, and their numbers were equal to those of the *hetaîroi*. (Marsyas/ Wikimedia Commons/ CC-BY-SA-3.0)

an awkward truth for Alexander, whose propaganda had attempted to sell his campaign as a Pan-Hellenic crusade against the common enemy of the Greeks. In reality, for the Persian empire the reliance upon the hoplite was to increase as the 4th century BC progressed, so much so that Dareios III

Marble grave stele (Paris, Musée du Louvre, inv. Ma 836) from the Thessalian *polis* of Pelinnaîon, central Greece, dated 350/340 BC. The horseman wears a Phrygian helmet, fabric body armour known as a *linothōrax*, and a *chlamýs* pinned with a *fibula* at the right shoulder. (Tangopaso/ Wikimedia Commons/ Public domain)

reckoned that 100,000 troops should be enough to conduct his forthcoming war against Alexander as long as 'a third were Greek mercenaries' (Diod. 17.30.3). After all, at Kounaxa (401 BC) the victory had been won for Kyros the Younger by the Greek mercenaries. More to the point, many Greeks simply viewed Macedonia a greater threat to Greece than Persia.

The quick character sketch of the Athenian Charidēmos penned by Curtius is a good case in point: 'an experienced soldier with a grudge against Alexander because of his exile (it was Alexander's command that he had been expelled from Athens)' (3.2.10, cf. Arr. *Anab.* 1.10.3–6, Plut. *Dem.* 23.4–6). It is a shame Curtius did not have more to say about the brilliant career of this lowborn outsider and footloose adventurer, who began as a slinger from Euboia in a war against Athens, and became in turn a pirate chief, mercenary captain, son-in-law to a Thracian chieftain, citizen and *stratēgós* of Athens (Dem. 23.148–51). He ultimately washed up as a refugee at the court and camp of Dareios III. Diodoros Siculus called Charidēmos 'a man admired for his courage and strategic genius' (17.30.2). He was candid too. On the eve of the battle of Issos, in 333 BC, Charidēmos dared to criticize the Great King and his tactics. You do not have to know very much, if anything at all, about Charidēmos' career to know that the next event was his own execution (Curt. 3.2.17–18). Speaking truth to power, what the Athenians called *parrhēssía*, can be an extremely risky business, particularly so when that power is absolute and in the iron grip of a touchy tyrant.

Having butchered nearly 18,000 Greek mercenaries that were in the pay of Dareios, the surviving 2,000 were sent bound in chains to Macedonia so they could end their lives as slaves (Arr. *Anab.* 1.16.6 with 14.4, cf. Plut. *Mor.* 181b, *Alex.* 16.6–7). Clearly Alexander wished to make an example of these men, especially as he was armed with the mandate of the League of Corinth, which meant as the *hēgemōn* of the Greek allies he could legally treat any Greek who stood against him as a traitor to Greece. Once the Great King had been removed from the game, however, such high principles were soon forgotten.

Alexander, after receiving the unconditional surrender of the surviving hoplite mercenaries in the pay of the Great King, simply discharged those Greeks who had enlisted in Persian service prior to the establishment of the League of Corinth, while the remainder were hired at the customary rates of pay (Diod. 17.76.2, Curt. 6.5.8–10, Arr. *Anab.* 3.24.5, cf. 2.3.8–9). Florid

Boiotian helmet (Oxford, Ashmolean Museum, AN1977.256) recovered from the Tigris, Iraq. It is believed to have been lost by one of Alexander's horsemen. It has eyelets for cord strapping. Modelled on a folded-down Boiotian variant of the *petasos*, a broad-brimmed sun hat, this type of helmet was beaten from a single sheet of bronze using a limestone former. As an open helmet, it allowed good peripheral vision and unimpaired hearing. It had a domed skull surrounded by a wide, flaring, downward sloping brim. The fluted brim came down at the rear to protect the neck and projected forward over the forehead. For cavalry use it had the advantage that the face was open and the wearer could hear commands without difficulty. Xenophon (b. *c.* 428 BC), Athenian well-bred horseman and down-at-heel soldier of fortune, considered 'the Boiotian pattern the most satisfactory' (*PH* 12.3) for horsemen. This piece of sound advice was taken up by Alexander, so replacing the Phrygian style used by Macedonian horsemen in his father's day. (Gts-tg/Wikimedia Commons/CC-BY-SA-4.0)

hypocrisy, not plain morality, often finds a place in the seedy underbelly of high politics, and the malevolent tendency to overlook transgressions for the sake of political usefulness has not gone anywhere. Mercenaries (as commonly defined) are generally individuals serving in foreign combat roles. Such instruments are necessary, but are undoubtedly dangerous, but they have one useful quality, that they can be abandoned in case of need. To borrow a quote from William Tecumseh Sherman, 'War is cruelty and you cannot refine it'. Alexander himself was almost certainly aware of the following Greek adage: 'For, as the proverb has it, the experiment should be made "on the worthless Karian" not on the *stratēgós*' (Polyb. 10.32.11). Ephoros of Kyme (*FGrHist* 70 F12), who wrote in the 4th century BC, believed that the Karians were the first foreign mercenary fighters to serve for payment; they certainly make an appearance as such in the Bible (2 Kings 11:4). Non-Hellenic Karia had a wide reputation as a supplier of hoplite mercenaries (Archil. fr. 216 West, Hdt. 2.152, Diod. 1.66.12, Strab. 14.2.28, Ael. *NA* 12.30, Plut. *Mor.* 302a) who hired themselves out to go in harm's way, so risking their necks for the sake of others by doing their 'dirty work' for them.

Dirty war

According to Plutarch (*Dem.* 20.2) the eloquent Demosthenes was also present at Chairōneia – probably serving as a citizen hoplite in the Athenian phalanx – and is said to have run away, casting aside his panoply as he scuttled back to Athens. By and large the military profile of Philip's army was

In Persian *panj* is five and *āb* is water, thus the land where five rivers flow south to finally join the Indus was known as the Punjab: from west to east, the Jhelum, the Chenāb, the Rāvī, the Beās, and the Sutlej. This is the Chenāb, which the Greeks knew as the Akesínēs, which formed the eastern boundary of the Paurava lands, the kingdom of Poros. His kingdom, like that of Āmbhi of Taxila, was nominally part of the Persian empire and paid tribute. In the *Mahābhārata* the common name of the river was Chandrabhaga because the river is formed from the confluence of two rivers, the Chandra and the Bhaga. (Sair18791/Wikimedia Commons/CC-BY-SA-4.0)

as Demosthenes himself so aptly describes it when he had previously railed at an audience of complacent Athenians:

> But for my own part, while practically all the arts have made a great advance and we are living today in a very different world from the old one, I consider that nothing has been more revolutionized and improved than the art of war. For in the first place I am informed that in those days the Lakedaimonians [Spartans], like everyone else, would spend four or five months of the summer season in invading and laying waste the enemy's territory with hoplites and levies of citizens, and would retire home again; and they were so old-fashioned, or rather such good citizens, that they never used money to buy an advantage from anyone, but their fighting was of the fair and open kind. On the other hand you hear of Philip marching unchecked, not because he leads a phalanx of hoplites, but because skirmishers, cavalry, archers, mercenaries, and similar troops accompany him. When, relying on this force, he attacks some people that is at variance with itself, and when through distrust no one goes forth to fight for his state, he brings up his artillery and lays siege. I need hardly tell you that he makes no difference between summer and winter and has no season set apart for inaction. (Dem. 9.47–51)

Notwithstanding Demosthenes' outright hostility to Philip, and of course the orator is enjoying the kind of grand, sweeping tones that built his career, these statements do ring true. The old constraints of time and space in agrarian warfare were irrelevant to the king and so were swept away. His army fought all year round, regardless of terrain, weather or distance, seeking out the enemy so as to bring him to battle. And when his army fought, it shattered the cohesion of the enemy, before destroying them in the pursuit.[5] These changes, however, bothered the conservative Greeks of the *polis*, who still clung to the idea that military service meant a mass collision of citizen hoplites during the brief summer campaigning season, and thus something one-dimensional and quasi-ritualistic that transcended killing the enemy in battle.

---

5   In the words of Clausewitz, 'Next to victory, the act of pursuit is most important in war' (*Principles of War*, II.3.7b, cf. III.1.8).

The land of five waters: the Punjab

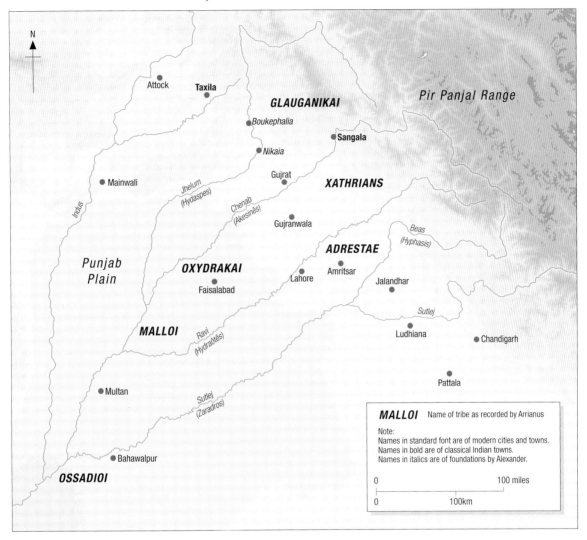

POROS' ARMY

> A raja relies mainly on elephants for achieving victory in battles. With their very large bodies, they are able to do things in war which are dangerous for other arms of the forces; they can be used to crush the enemy's foot soldiers, battle arrays, forts and encampments.
>
> Kauṭilya *AS* 2.2.13, 14

The army of Poros was a traditional Indian army that harked back to the art of warfare described in the epic poem *Mahābhārata*, one of the founding epics of Indian culture. This recalls the heroic battles in an age anterior to that of Alexander and the Mauryas, a distant past when mighty warriors fought alongside the Hindu warrior gods. It is certain, however, that when Alexander invaded India standing armies had become a regular feature of Indian kingdoms and states. As such, an army was supplied by the

The war of the Buddha's relics, lowest architrave, South Gateway, Great Stūpa (No. 1), Sāñchī. This richly carved gateway (*toraṇa*) is the oldest and main entrance to the stūpa (Marshall 1918: 37). In the centre of the architrave, the siege of Kusinārā, the capital of the Mallas, is in full swing, a scene dominated by men armed with long cane bows, the weapon closely associated with classical Indian warriors and which tallies with the eyewitness account of Nearkhos of Crete. To right and left, the victorious chiefs of the seven other clans are departing in their chariots at the head of their armies. The relics are borne on the heads of the war elephants. This relief is one of the earliest representations of the 'fourfold' army containing foot warriors, horsemen, chariots and elephants. Drums and pipes accompany them. The reliefs at Sāñchī indicate that war gear changed little over the classical Indian period and beyond. (Asitjain/Wikimedia Commons/ CC-BY-SA-3.0)

government with the necessary equipment and supplies and always remained at its disposal and command.

The *Mahābhārata* sets up the traditional elements of the 'fourfold' army, collectively known as *caturanga-bala* or *caturanga-camū* (*Mbh* 3.17.2, 4.63.13, 5.19.1, 30.25, 7.19.15, 8.15.11, 9.8.2, 22.84), that is to say, the four arms of the Indian army made up of foot soldiers (*patti*), horsemen, war chariots (*rathins*), and war elephants. Kauṭilya (e.g. *AS* 2.33.9, 9.1.2, 10.4.15) still proposes the classical Indian 'fourfold' as the ideal division of the army in his day, in which the four arms were meant to work together, in various roles, to produce the best outcome. The earliest representation of the 'fourfold' army is met in the Sāñchī reliefs (Marshall 1918: pl. Vb). Even when war chariots, which had been the main strength of the epic army, fell out of use finally in the 7th century AD, the four-arms classification would remain so until the following century, a time when Hindu armies were fighting the invading armies of Islam.

Foot warriors

Providing the bulk of Indian armies, Indian foot warriors, according to the personal observation of Megasthenēs, were paid and maintained, owing hereditary duty to their ruler, but 'when not engaged in active service, pass their time in idleness and drinking' (*Indiká* fr. 33 apud Strab. 15.1.47). In a similar vein, Arrianus says of these warriors: 'They have only military duties to perform … As long as they are required to fight, they fight; and when peace returns, they abandon themselves to enjoyment' (*Ind.* 12.4). Contrary to perceived wisdom that they were excluded from military service, it was the two lowest *varṇas*, *viśayas* and *śūdras*, who generally constituted the rank and file of an Indian army. In the *Arthaśāstra* (9.2.21), though *kṣatriyas* are more proficient in the military arts, Kauṭilya expressly approves of a large army composed of *viśayas* ('cultivators') and *śūdras* ('toilers'). He also says (ibid. 8.5.1) two of the primary causes that breed discontent and trouble in an army are the arrears of pay and the irregularity of rations.

Foot warriors wore no more than a linen or cotton cloth in the fashion of a kilt, gathered at the front, and most of the written sources confirm the skimpiness of their battle attire, with phrases like 'naked and barefooted', 'nearly naked', and 'bare from the waist up' being common. This is also seen in the sculpture of the period. When they geared up for war, as well as a broad-bladed sword, which was not less than three cubits (1.37m) in length according to the eyewitness Nearkhos (*FGrHist* 133 F11 apud Arr. *Ind.* 16.9), the majority of them carried a stout cane self-bow as tall as the wielder.

Herodotos (7.65) speaks of the arrows of Indian warriors tipped with iron, while Kauṭilya mentions arrowheads 'made of iron, bone or wood as to cut, rend or pierce' (*AS* 2.18.11). The reed arrows themselves were extremely long – Curtius says 'two cubits long' (9.5.9), Arrianus 'a little short of three cubits' (*Ind.* 16.7) – and are described as inflicting serious deep wounds at close range and even capable of penetrating armour. Alexander himself was to suffer a chest wound and punctured lung after one of these arrows had punched through his armour (Plut. *Alex.* 63.3, Arr. *Anab.* 6.10.1).

Both Arrianus (*Ind.* 16.6) and Curtius (8.14.19) reckon that because the bow was as long as the man who bore it was tall, the bowman had to brace his long heavy bow with his left foot when he loosed his arrows. Though such bracing is not depicted in the Indian reliefs of the period, the obvious drawback of this massive bow was its unwieldiness, and the fact that damp and muddy conditions would affect the tension of the lengthy sinew or hemp bowstring, as did happen at the Hydaspes (Curt. 8.14.19). One Indian captive, apparently 'a man who had the greatest repute for marksmanship', preferred death rather than risk failure when challenged by Alexander to 'send an arrow through a ringer-ring' (Plut. *Mor.* 181b). The arrows themselves were housed in a quiver worn vertically down the centre of the back, suspended by cross belts. Bowmen did not carry shields, though

Three Indian warriors, upper register of the tomb of Xerxes I (r. 486–465 BC), Nāqš-e Rostām, which represent the Achaemenid Persian domains in the Punjāb. Cyrus (r. 558–530 BC) conquered Gandhāra (OP *Gadāra*), while Dareios I (r. 522–486 BC) annexed the region of Taxila (OP *Hidūš*). Indian warriors 'dressed in cotton; they carried cane bows and cane arrows tipped with iron' (Hdt. 7.65) joined Xerxes' expeditionary army of 480 BC. Though not intended as individualized portraits, these three are wearing what Indians wear, the cotton cloth in the fashion of a kilt, gathered at the front, and carry the broad bladed sword much favoured by Indian warriors. (A.Davey/Wikimedia Commons/CC-BY-SA-2.0)

Statue of Bhīma's iron-clad mace, Thrippuliyoor Mahavishnu Temple, Puliyoor, Kerala. Bhīma, among other epic heroes, excelled in the use of this fearsome bludgeoning weapon, and in epic tradition the mace (*gadā*) is more important than the sword and used by nobles and commoners alike. Made of wood or metal, it consisted essentially of a spherical head mounted on a shaft, with a spike on the top. The mace remained a battlefield weapon at the time of Alexander. When he attacked the capital of the Malloi, Alexander, already transfixed by an arrow, 'received a blow on the neck from a mace which forced him to lean against the wall, although he still faced his assailants' (Plut. *Alex*. 63.4). (Alexinov/Wikimedia Commons/CC-BY-SA-4.0)

they did wear leather bracers to protect their bow arm from the friction of the bowstring, and they may have worn some form of protection for the fingers too, probably leather fingerstalls sewn to corresponding straps (*AS* 2.18).

Other foot warriors are said to have carried light shields of undressed ox hide, two-handed swords and javelins. Kauṭilya (*AS* 2.18.17) mentions cane, bamboo, wood and hide as the materials for the fabrication of shields. These shields are nearly as tall as the wielder but narrow, and were principally to protect against incoming arrows. Kauṭilya says (*AS* 10.5.37) that in an array of foot warriors, the men with the shields should stand in front of the bowmen. This leads us to the observation made by Arrianus (*Ind*. 16.9) when he says that Indian bowmen preferred the comparative security of loosing arrows from a distance rather than engaging with their broad-bladed swords. He adds that when they did reluctantly engage in hand-to-hand combat, they wielded their swords with both hands to unleash a weighty downward cutting stroke.

Indian swords were of good iron with hilts of rhinoceros and buffalo horn, elephant tusk, wood or bamboo root (*AS* 2.18.13). In the epics scabbards are commonly made of cowhide, goatskin or tigerskin (e.g. *Mbh* 4.38.30, 32, 33). At Bhārhut and Sāñchī scabbards are shown suspended from the left shoulder by means of a broad strap. The renowned crucible or wootz steel had its origins in southern India and Sri Lanka, probably at the turn of the 5th century BC. Ktēsiās of Knidos, in his *Indiká* (*FGrHist* 668 F45.9.8–15), praises the two swords of superb quality, made of Indian steel, which were presented to him by Artaxerxes II Mnēmōn (r. 404–358 BC) and the queen mother Parysatis during his stay at the Persian court as private physician to the Great King. Curtius (9.8.1) refers to a hundred talents of Indian steel presented to Alexander by the Malloi and Sudracae.

Horsemen

The horsemen appear to be the weakest arm of an Indian army. The horses were overfed and occasionally dosed with wine to dull their tempers. Their battlefield role was the 'supervision of the discipline of the army; lengthening the line of the army; protecting the sides of the army; first attack' and the like (*AS* 10.4.13). It is intriguing to note that one of their most important tasks was policing the army. Nonetheless, it was appreciated that two of their important roles were scouting and the pursuit of the enemy.

In battle, horsemen 'move at a measured pace and in a straight course'. They were mostly unarmoured and armed with two short spears and a shield (Arr. *Ind*. 16.10). In some of the Ajantā cave paintings the spears are depicted as short, with triangular blades and ferules. Indian horsemen rode with just a saddlecloth, which could be elaborately decorated. Arrianus also records that horses were controlled by a leather noseband, studded on the inside with bronze, iron or ivory spikes. The bit was a simple iron mouthpiece, 'like a spit', connected to the reins and the noseband, and the spikes of the latter served to reinforce the action of the bit (Arr. *Ind*.

Caturanga (Osaka, National Museum of Ethnology, inv. MI 0186) from Rajasthan, India. An ancient Indian strategy game, the form of chess brought to late-mediaeval Europe. In *caturanga* there is a king (*raja*), a councillor (*mantra*), two elephants (*gajas*), two horses (*aşvas*), two chariots (*rathas*), and eight foot warriors (*padātis*), played on a game board divided into an 8x8 grid of squares know as the *aşţāpada*. In the *Ŗgveda* the word *caturanga* means 'four-limbed' with reference to the human body; in later Hindu literature it is regularly used to denote the fourfold army of foot warriors, horsemen, chariots and elephants. (Yanajin33/Wikimedia Commons/CC-BY-CA-4.0)

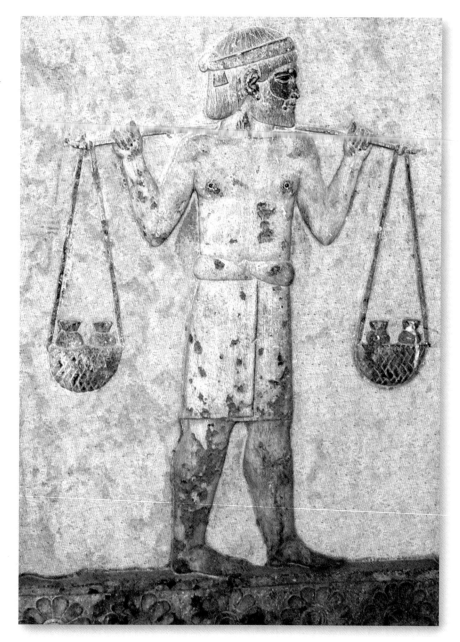

16.11–12). However, this does contradict the statement of Megasthenēs, who says that 'it is the practice with them [viz. the Indians] to control their horse with bit and bridle, and to make them move at a measured pace and in a straight course' (*Indiká* fr. 35 apud Ael. *NA* 13.10). Megasthenēs' testimony is supported by the Sānchī reliefs, which clearly depict the headgear of the horses at the time.

The *Mahābhārata* (2.25.19, 47.4, 48.23) mentions various horse hues, such as dark grey, 'pigeon-coloured', ivory white, piebald and red bay. In sculpture the horse's forelock is usually drawn up through a tube to act as a plume. Kauṭilya says that the best war horses 'came from Kāmboja, Sindhu, Āraṭṭa and Vanāyu' (*AS* 2.30.29), that is today's Afghanistan, Pakistan, Punjab, and the Arabian peninsula.

Charioteers

Charioteers (and elephant riders) were the elite of an Indian army. At the time of Alexander's successors, a standard of one war chariot (or elephant) to five horsemen and 15 foot warriors and 15 guards was reckoned a good ratio of troops (*AS* 10.5.12–13). Chariots were usually classified by size and Kauṭilya (ibid. 2.33.3, 4) delineates eight types ranging from light six-*puruṣas*- (1.40m) long chariots, to heavier ones measuring ten *puruṣas* (2.32m) in height and 12 *puruṣas* (2.74m) in length. The different sizes probably reflect the different numbers of crew, though which of these served as war chariots (*sāngrāmika*) is uncertain as Kauṭilya does not stipulate.

The Greek historians make it abundantly clear that in the age of Alexander the Indians placed their principal reliance in battle on elephants tamed and trained for the purpose. Poros, after all, came to the field of battle riding not a chariot but an elephant, and, as we shall see, at the Hydaspes his chariot arm failed miserably. In the epics, however, the chief strength of the army consisted of the chariot warriors. In Sāñchī we witness light chariots drawn

Front face, second panel of the left pillar, South Gateway, Great Stūpa (No. 1), Sāñchī. Aśōka (r. 268–231 BC) rides in his two-horse chariot accompanied by his retinue. The grandson of the dynasty's founder Chandragupta Maurya, Aśōka introduced Buddhism to Gandhāra, northwest India. Both Sri Lankan and north Indian traditions assert he was a vindictive man with an addiction to bloodshed before his conversion to Buddhism, allegedly through remorse at the carnage of his greatest victory. (Biswarup Ganguly/ Wikimedia Commons/ CC-BY-SA-3.0)

Sandstone pillar, temple of Bāla Krishna, Hampi, built by the Vijayanagara ruler Krishnadevaraya (r. 1509–29) in 1513. Warrior woman with a cane bow, upon which she leans while an attendant removes a thorn from her heel. A quiver of arrows is carved in shallow relief slung across her back. According to Nearkhos of Crete (apud Arr. *Ind.* 16.6) classical Indian warriors used a cane self-bow that equalled its wielder in height, precisely as depicted in this relief. Arrows were tipped with metal, bone or wood with the shaft of reed. By and large, the literary evidence, Indian or Greek, is confirmed by the available evidence of ancient and medieval Indian art. (G41m8/Wikimedia Commons/ CC-BY-SA-4.0)

by two horses and those in the epics were two-horse vehicles carrying a charioteer and a warrior.

By Alexander's time, however, chariots appear to have been drawn by four horses (two fastened to the pole by means of a double yoke, two by traces outside), and were crewed by one charioteer and two warriors. The latter could have any matter of body armour and weaponry, including gilded maces. The heroes of Indian epic fought in a variety of styles, but predominantly as archers riding in chariots. The famous battle hymn of the *Ṛgveda* (6.75) describes the *kṣatriya* on his chariot, armed with his bow and dressed in armour, with a bracer on his left arm to avoid the friction of the bowstring. The chariot warrior favoured the composite bow, its size suiting itself perfectly to use from a chariot. Skilled archers could shoot while moving through the length and breadth of the battlefield. In the epics they also had a passion for bows inlaid with glowing gold motifs such as elephants, little insects, and dots, and bow cases and quivers covered in tigerskin (*Mbh* 4.38.20).

Poros' four-horse chariots at the Hydaspes are described as having two charioteers armed with javelins, two warriors armed with bows, and two shield bearers to protect the others (Curt. 8.14.3, cf. 9.8.1). Such two-wheeled leviathans are not witnessed before or after the battle, and it has been suggested that the two shield bearers are actually escorts or runners. A commentary on the Buddhist scripture *Vinaya Piṭaka* refers to the war chariot of epic tradition as being followed by 'two wheel guards' (*cakra-rakṣau*: IV 105). The eyewitness evidence of Megasthenēs (*Indiká* fr. 34 apud Strab. 15.1.52), on the contrary, suggests four-horse chariots with two crewmen and one charioteer a short time after. Kauṭilya says that the main battlefield functions of chariots are 'protection of the army; repelling the attack made by all the four constituents of the enemy's army; seizing and abandoning (positions) during the time of battle; gathering a dispersed army; breaking the compact array of the enemy's army; frightening it; magnificence; and fearful noise' (*AS* 10.4.15). Success, of course, depended largely upon the mettle and dexterity of the charioteers. To be successful, however, they required even ground in ideal conditions: as Kauṭilya (ibid. 9.1.50, cf. 10.4.3, *Mbh* 12.24) makes clear, chariots work best in the dry season. The Hydaspes will demonstrate the futility of chariotry in mud and rain (Arr. *Anab.* 5.15.2, Curt. 8.14.4).

Chariots are described as ornate, especially around their edges, and are occasionally armoured along with their occupants. The rear of the cab would normally carry the personal banner of its noble occupant, a valuable rally point in battle. Bells were attached to chariots, and charioteers used conches to add to the tremendous din. Parasols (*chatras*) could cover the cabs (*Mbh* 3.230, 6.20.9, 7.135.46, etc.), and were trophies of great importance; to lose one's parasol or banner was considered quite dishonourable (ibid. 3.231.5, 4.52.22, 59.6, etc.).

Elephants

According to Megasthenēs, elephants (and horses) were 'held to be the special property of the king, and persons are appointed to take care of them' (*Indiká* fr. 36 apud Strab. 15.1.41). Arrianus adds that 'the elephant in India is a royal mount' (*Ind.* 17.2). Rightly so, as we have witnessed above with Poros.

In war the elephant's major function was to terrify the opposition, fear being the beast's strongest weapon, and to wreak as much destruction as possible. They were used in two basic ways on the battlefield: as a screen against horsemen, horses, unless specially trained, disliking the sight, sound and smell of elephants; and to attack infantry, not least because they offered a higher platform from which missiles could be launched (*AS* 10.4.14, 5.53–54). In these roles, however, the elephant was not conspicuously successful, and its offensive promise never lived up to expectations. A source of disaster and defeat, it was too vulnerable to missile weapons. It was also too slow. Indeed, well-trained infantry could successfully deal with elephants,

THE BATTLE OF THE HYDASPES

Like a snake swallowing up mice, the Earth swallows the raja who refuses to fight and the *brāhmaṇa* who is unduly attached to his wives and children.

Mbh 12.57.3

The upper Indus and Pīr-Sar (elev. 2,591m), viewed from the north. In April 1926 Aurel Stein suggested that the rock of Aornos (San. *Āvárana*, 'hiding place') was located on Pīr-Sar, a mountain spur above narrow gorges in a bend of the upper Indus. Despite arguments (Giuseppe Tuci, Luca Olivieri, Ernst Badian, etc.) identifying Aornos with Mount Illam, Megasthenēs (fr. 46 apud Strab. 15.1.8) and Diodoros Siculus (17.85.3) both say the foot of Aornos was washed by the Indus, while Curtius (8.11.7) writes that the river comes close to its base. Separating Swāt from Buner, Mount Illam is 40km west from the Indus. According to local legend, not even Lord Krishna – Diodoros Siculus (17.85.2) and Arrianus (4.28.1) identify him as Herakles (both share the attributes of animal skin and club/mace) – had been able to take the rock, which rose 1,700m above the Indus. Regardless of sub-zero conditions, Alexander forced his way up with dismantled siege equipment on donkeys. The taking of Aornos made no real military sense (*contra* Fuller 1989: 127), but from a psychological point of view the message was clear: resistance was futile, for the Indians were facing the *avatar* of a god greater than the divine hero Lord Krishna, whose exploits are famously recounted in the *Mahābhārata*. (Jona Lendering/ Livius.org/CC0 1.0 Universal)

A venture that had been maturing in his mind since at least the summer of 328 BC (Arr. *Anab.* 4.15.6), Alexander was to inaugurate his invasion of India by what can only be described as a campaign of terror. In what appeared to be a coordinated operation, fire and sword was visited upon the warlike tribes that inhabited the mountainous regions of what is now the Swat Valley in the North-West Frontier of Pakistan. It has been suggested by some scholars that the suppression of these people was done in order to secure his lines of communication into the Indian Subcontinent. That may be so. But a more cogent reason for this death and destruction can be put down to Alexander's violent longing, his *póthos*.

In any case, after fierce fighting at a number of local citadels, the climax of which was the taking of the natural feature rising precipitously above the Indus called Aornos, Alexander headed to a prearranged rendezvous point with Perdikkas and Hēphaistiōn. These two companions of Alexander had been earlier despatched over what is now the Khyber Pass and down towards the Indus with orders to bridge the river. The former Persian empire did

The last campaign: Alexander's route to the Hydaspes

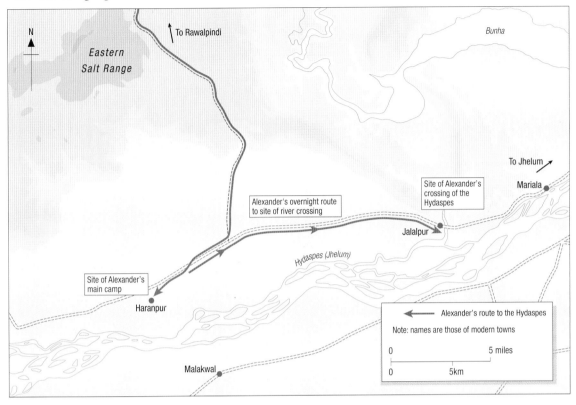

once stretch as far east as the Indus, but it had long since ceased to before Alexander's arrival upon the world stage. Having crossed the Indus, the old Persian frontier, Alexander marched his reunited army to Taxila, where the Macedonian king was warmly welcomed. It was early spring 326 BC.

At some point Poros had written to Alexander, according to the *Metz Epitome*, a communiqué that ended with the following brave words: 'I shall do only one thing that you demand – to be ready and waiting for you, in arms, at my borders' (*Metz Epit.* 57). Apparently the Macedonian had ordered the Indian 'to present himself to him at the boundaries of his kingdom' (ibid. 55). Curtius has a similar story whereby Poros vigorously answers the Macedonian's ultimatum by promising 'he would be present when Alexander entered his kingdom – but he would be under arms' (8.13.2). The size and strength of the foreign army was an unknown quantity and would be so until its arrival. However, the raja knew the land and the invaders did not – they would be seeing it for the first time – and he felt confident that he could prevent the Macedonian king from crossing the Hydaspes and occupying his kingdom. In the event, he was proved wrong.

In May 326 BC Alexander, with his new ally Āmbhi of Taxila in tow along with 5,000 of his Indians (Arr. *Anab.* 5.8.5), left Taxila and marched towards the Hydaspes.[6] Their objective was to confront and overcome the forces of

---

6   According to Arrianus, the battle was fought in 'the month of Mounychiòn' (5.19.3), which equates to 18 April to 18 May. Diodoros Siculus (17.87.1) wrongly assigns the battle to the archonship of Chremes, i.e. July 326 BC to June 325 BC. According to the eyewitness Nearkhos (apud Strab. 15.1.18, Arr. *Ind.* 6.5) at the summer solstice (i.e. around 21 July) Alexander was encamped on the Akesínes.

Remains of a bastion and circuit wall, part of the Nandana fortress, raised on an abrupt rocky ridge commanding the pass at the eastern end of the Salt Range, Punjab province of Pakistan. Barring the descent on the zig-zagging route through the pass, Nandana remained an important stronghold of the Hindu Shāhiya dynasty until it was ousted by Mahmūd Ghaznavi (1014), who had vowed a *jihad* against the idolaters of India (he invaded the Subcontinent 17 times). The pass was used by a later great invader of India, Bābur, a descendent of Temūr-i Lang and founder of the Mughal dynasty (r. 1526–30), when he made his first inroads into the Punjab across the Salt Range, reaching as far as the Chenāb River (1519). As ably demonstrated by Aurel Stein, Alexander's army almost certainly passed through here as it made its way south towards the Hydaspes. (Omarjhawarian/Wikimedia Commons/CC-BY-SA-3.0)

The Indus at Hund, Swab District, Pakistan. Arrianus describes the formidable Indus as 'bigger than any river in Europe' (*Anab.* 5.2, cf. 5.6.11). Known in antiquity as Udabhandapura, Hund was the site of Alexander's crossing of this fast-flowing waterway at the close of his expedition against Aornos. At a place where the ruined fort built by the Mughal emperor Jalal ud-Din Akbar (r. 1556–1605) now overlooks the river, Alexander's military engineers, led by the Thessalian Diades and under the overall command of Hēphaistiōn and Perdikkas, were to construct a bridge of boats according to Arrianus (using the Roman method of his own day as an analogy). Before the Grand Trunk Road shifted about 25km downstream to Attock during the Mughal period, this was the crossing place of the Indus on the ancient road from Central Asia to India and beyond. (Ahmad Faraz22/Wikimedia Commons/CC-BY-SA-4.0)

Poros. None of the main literary sources provide much of a clue regarding the route that Alexander took from Taxila. Arrianus, for instance, has Alexander quitting Taxila only to instantly appear on the right bank of the Hydaspes.

According to the elder Pliny (6.21 §62), the distance between Taxila and the Hydaspes, as measured by Alexander's surveyors Diognētos and Baitōn, was 120 Roman miles (177.58km), whereas Strabo says 'the direction of march, as far as the Hydaspes, was for the most part towards the south' (15.1.32). These two snippets of information agree with the route Taxila–Nandana–Haranpur proposed by the explorer and archaeologist Marc Aurel Stein (1862–1943), the last location (a large village in Stein's day, now a

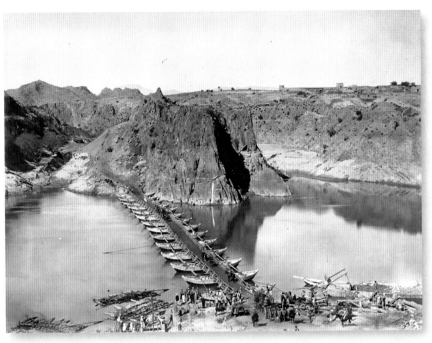

town) being where Alexander established his main camp close to the right bank of the Hydaspes (Stein 1937: 27). His work on Alexander's trail is now accepted as the most plausible analysis of that long-ago campaign. From Taxila Alexander travelled south to what are now Chautra, Chakwal and Kallar Kahar to descend from the Salt Range via the Nandana Pass, a natural and narrow cleft in the hills. Once on the river plain he turned downriver along the Hydaspes to establish his main camp at Haranpur.

The Indian warrior king was obviously resolute in his resolve to face the foreign invader and his traditional enemy, Āmbhi, and prevent their armed advance into his realm, the Paurava lands. To this end Poros made his intentions plain by mustering a sizeable local army, including a large number of Indian war elephants (Arr. *Anab.* 5.15.5 = 200, Diod. 18.87.2 = 130, Curt. 8.13.6 and *Metz Epit.* 54 = 85) placed in full view on the left bank of the fast-flowing Hydaspes. This considerable waterway (unlike the comparatively modest rivers Granīkos or Pinaros) had already begun to rise and broaden with the heavy glacial run-off from the Himalayas – Curtius says the river was now 'four *stadia* [0.74km] wide' and 'presented the appearance of a vast sea' (8.13.8) – and would rise and broaden still more with the advent of the monsoon season at the summer solstice. With the force of nature on his side, it comes as no surprise to learn that Poros 'was determined either to prevent Alexander from crossing or to attack him if he tried to cross' (Arr. *Anab.* 5.8.4). As Alexander descended the eastern escarpments of what is now known as the Salt Range, he found Poros' 'fourfold' army of foot warriors, horsemen, chariots and elephants arrayed on the left bank of the Hydaspes.

More than its daily rising waters, it was Poros' elephants that made a straightforward crossing of the river impracticable. The quandary for Alexander was that he needed his horsemen for a pitched battle. On the other hand, he appreciated that as soon as his horses sensed the terrifying presence of these larger-than-life leviathans, they would become frantic when in the water or on their rafts, making it impossible to land them on the far

The eastern end of the Salt Range, Punjab province of Pakistan. The range extends along the southern edge of a fold-and-thrust belt that underlies the Pothohar Plateau and the north of the Jhelum. The furthest tendrils of the Himalayas, the range derives its name from its extensive deposits of rock salt, the table salt with a distinctive pink hue (due to dozens of trace minerals) known as Himalayan salt. Local legend traces the discovery of Himalayan salt deposits to the army of Alexander when its horses started licking the rocks. (Khalid Mahmood/Wikimedia Commons/CC-BY-SA-3.0)

side of the river in any sort of coherent formation. Even his soldiers were rather intimidated by them. He needed to find a way to convey a part of his army across the continuing swelling river without attracting the enemy's attention, allowing these troops the crucial element of surprise and the necessary breathing space to collect themselves before battle was joined.

First, however, Alexander needed to convince Poros that he intended to wait until the dry season, by which time the waters of the Hydaspes would have receded. To this end, he spread flying rumours to that effect. Moreover, he plundered the countryside so as to accumulate a vast store of provender. Likewise, he settled his troops in quarters (Arr. *Anab.* 5.9.3–4). Yet as Arrianus writes, Alexander 'continued to watch for an opening nonetheless, in the hope that he might somehow steal across swiftly without being detected' (ibid. 10.1). The Macedonian conqueror had no intention of rotting in a sodden camp until the rains abated sometime in September and the river became fordable once more. So much for the long wait that Poros had anticipated.

THE CROSSING

> If the crossing point has been seized by the enemy, the army shall cross the water at another point at night and then ambush the enemy [from his rear].
>
> Kauṭilya AS 10.2.14

Principally, what Kauṭilya counsels is entangling the enemy in an ambuscade by forcing the river elsewhere if said enemy is holding the key crossing point. In a purely Indian context, this can be illustrated by the encounter of the Ten Kings (San. *dāśarājñá*), a battle between Sudās Paijavana, tribal chieftain of the Bharatas, and a confederation of neighbouring northern tribes. Both contending parties planned to ford the Beās (then the Vipāśá) and the Sutlej

(then the Śutudrī) to pull off a surprise attack. But the confederation took the initiative and overwhelmed the opposition on the left bank of the Rāvī (then the Paruṣṇī) near a place called Mānuṣa, west of Kurukṣetra,[7] in an ambuscade, making it impossible for Sudās to escape (*RV* 7.18.5–21). This stratagem was to be adopted by Alexander in crossing the Hydaspes, seeing that Poros guarded the accustomed passage with his army arrayed for battle.

Because of the rapidly rising waters of the Hydaspes, time for Alexander was not a limitless luxury. Clearly, however, the crossing of the broad and rapid river could prove disastrous if done so in the teeth of the enemy. Assault river crossings are intrinsically dangerous, and at the Hydaspes the Indians had two tactical options. They could time their strike on the Macedonians at their most vulnerable: midstream. This option would rely on the use of missile fire, an asset the Indians had aplenty. An alternative, if they chose to wait, was to overwhelm the leading Macedonian elements as they laboured to maintain a precarious foothold at the disembarkation point. Obviously this option meant closing with the enemy, but it did have the benefit of falling upon them while they were wet and winded and still had their backs against the river. In both scenarios, the Indian strike would fall while the enemy had not yet assembled his forces and was restricted to a narrow space on the riverbank. Alexander needed to force a crossing unimpeded and then defeat the enemy on his terms.

To achieve his desired aim, Alexander personally chose a crossing point a full day's march upriver from his main camp, a distance of 150 *stadia* (27.5km) according to Arrianus (*Anab.* 5.11.2, cf. Frontin. 1.4.9a). The complex preparations prior to the crossing were accomplished with the aid of numerous feints and other nefarious deceptions. These included noisily marching his troops up and down his side of the river each and every day, the Indians vigilantly shadowing these movements. Apparently, there was

The Grand Trunk Road crossing the Jhelum at the city of Jhelum. Covering a distance of 2,700km, the road runs through parts of Afghanistan, Pakistan, India, and Bangladesh, extending from Kabul to Chittagong via the Khyber Pass, Lahore, Delhi and Kolkata. The Indian-born Englishman Rudyard Kipling, who knew a few things about the North-West Frontier, called the Grand Trunk Road 'a river of life as nowhere else exists in the world' (*Kim* [New York, 1897], ch. 3, p. 94). Strabo talks (15.1.11) of a royal road with a length of 10,000 *stadia*, some 1,850km, which was probably the Grand Trunk Road of those days. The elder Pliny (6.21) adds that along its route markers were placed at every ten *stadia*. (Uzairr sajid/Wikimedia Commons/CC-BY-SA-4.0)

---

7   The field of Kurukṣetra was of course the setting for the battle between the Kauravas and the Pāṇḍavas that raged for 18 days, sometimes in favour of one side and sometimes in favour of the other.

Possible site of where Alexander forced the passage of the Hydaspes at the foot of what is today Jalālpur Sharif. Strabo (15.1.29, cf. Plut. *Alex.* 61, Arr. *Anab.* 5.19.4) places the site of Boukephalía, the city founded by Alexander in memory of his much-loved horse Boukephálas, at the point where he embarked for his pre-dawn crossing of the Hydaspes, that is, on the right bank of the river. It is believed to be located below or close to Jalālpur Sharif. If so, then this Pakistani town marks the furthest eastern end of his empire. Boukephalía itself was settled with Macedonian, Greek and Persian veterans and Pauravas locals. (Jona Lending & Marco Prins/Wikimedia Commons/ CC0 1.0 Universal)

also the ploy of a 'royal double' standing before the royal tent with all the necessary royal trappings (Curt. 8.13.20–21). As a result, Poros was kept continuously on his toes, until he decided it was all bluff and so relaxed his vigilance. The Indians had been lulled into a languid lethargy. Alexander was now ready.

Leaving Krateros, who now filled Parmeniōn's shoes, with a substantial Macedonian contingent and the Indian allies (Arr. *Anab.* 5.11.3), Alexander quietly drew the portion of his army earmarked for the crossing upriver. According to Arrianus (*Anab.* 5.14.1), this select force consisted of some 5,000 horsemen and 6,000 foot soldiers. As night always confers a crucial tactical advantage, the extensive preparations for forcing the river, which should never be taken for granted, were to unfold under the cover of darkness. Moreover, chance (or the gods) lent a helping hand in the guise of a violent thunderstorm (Plut. *Alex.* 60.2): though Alexander lost several men struck by lightning, it drowned out the various telltale noises of the assembling and embarking of the crossing force (Arr. *Anab.* 5.12.3).

Undated photograph (Washington, DC, Smithsonian Institution Archives, image no. SIA2008-2905) of a flotilla of skin rafts on the Huang He (Yellow River), the main river of northern China. Alexander's soldiers employed comparable rafts of straw-filled hides, which they doubtless steered with poles, to make the passage across the Hydaspes. The hides, probably sheep or goat, would have been tied with lengths of moistened leather cord that shrank and tightened as they dried, creating permanent seals. (Smithsonian Institution/ Public domain)

The Macedonians forced the actual crossing just before dawn as the rains began to ease. This they did by employing boats and wooden rafts buoyed up with straw-stuffed hides sewn up so as to be watertight (Polyain. 4.3.9). The latter technique had been used previously by Alexander's men when they crossed the Ister (Arr. *Anab*. 1.3.6), the Oxus (ibid. 3.29.4) and the Jaxartes (ibid. 4.4.2). The detailed description by Polybios (3.46.1–6) of those rafts made for ferrying Hannibal's elephants across the Rhodanós (Rhône) River indicates they were perhaps of a comparable construction to those used to ferry Alexander's horses. In 1838 and 1839, Helmuth von Moltke der Ältere, then a *Hauptmann* (captain) serving as an adviser to the Ottoman army, led a pair of expeditions down the upper Euphrates. In doing so he employed what were known as *kelleks* since the days of the Assyrians supported by inflated animal skins. The future Prussian field marshal was certainly impressed with this inflatable technology of yesteryear:

> Such a vehicle bends like a fish and assumes the shape of the wave on which it floats, by curving upwards or downwards. It suffers no harm when it is showered with water, momentarily sinking, and the most violent race against cliffs and rock tips tear at most one or a few tubes.[8]

The boats employed were those had been used for the earlier crossing of the Indus. These had been cut into sections and carted overland to the Hydaspes and reassembled (Arr. *Anab*. 5.12.3–4). Alexander himself embarked on a 30-oared vessel and crossed with, besides Perdikkas and Hēphaistíōn, Ptolemaios, Lysimakhos and Seleukos, three future kings (ibid. 13.1).

Though unchallenged, the crossing was not without its share of drama. Alexander put ashore on what he believed was the left bank of the Hydaspes. Actually, he had landed on what was a long, narrow island. Macedonian scouting may have been at fault, or the overnight deluge might have cut a new channel in the fast-flowing river. The bulk of his men were ashore before the mistake was realized and there was no time to re-embark. The Macedonians would have to ford the channel in full flood. The horses

---

8 Moltke, H. von, *Briefe über Zustande und Begobenheiten in der Tirkei au den Jahren 1835 bis 1839* (Berlin, 1876), pp. 360–63.

The small town of Jalālpur Sharif, south-west of the city of Jhelum, Punjab province of Pakistan, the possible location of the lost tomb of Boukephálas. The town sits on rising ground at the foot of a protecting spur of the Salt Range on the right bank of the Jhelum, which can be seen to the right, middle ground. The ruins of an ancient city are apparently spread across the foothills of the Salt Range to the west of Jalālpur Sharif. Coins found in the vicinity include issues dating back to the Diadochoi and the Greek kings who held sway over parts of what are now Afghanistan and the north-west of the Punjab. (franek2/Wikimedia Commons/CC-BY-SA-3.0)

crossed with little more than their heads above the rushing waters, while the men somehow managed to struggle onto dry land. They quickly formed up behind a screen formed by horse archers (Arr. *Anab.* 5.13.4) – these were Sakae and Dahae according to Curtius (8.14.5), most likely recruited during Alexander's Central Asian campaign. It is when things are going wrong that leadership is truly tested; it is easy to lead when things are going well.

Regarding the actual location that Alexander ultimately selected for his planned river crossing, on this we are informed by Arrianus:

> From the bank of the Hydaspes projected headland (ἄκρα/*ákra*), where the river made a considerable bend; it was thick with every sort of tree, and opposite was an island in the river, wooded and desolate, untrodden as it was by the foot of man. (Arr. *Anab.* 5.11.1)

So, the spot was an upstream bend, where a headland and wooded island would screen Alexander's river crossing. As a result of his extensive exploration of the area, Aurel Stein opined that this was the island 'occupied by the hamlet of Admana and some scattered homesteads belonging to it' (1932: 42).[9] Here the foothills of the Salt Range come right down to the river plain to form a promontory, Arrianus' *ákra*. Furthermore, Curtius adds that the island where Alexander crossed was not only wooded but also larger

9   The village of Admana exists to this day, and currently its population stands at 220 souls.

than the rest of the numerous islands in the river, and the author provides us with an addition detail:

> There was also a very deep ravine (*fossa praealta*) close to the bank which he commanded, and this could conceal not only his infantry but even men on horseback. (Curt. 8.13.17)

Remote and well hidden, this natural feature is what the locals call *nālā*, a deep torrent bed cut into the mountains by a seasonal watercourse. Identified by Aurel Stein as the Kandar Kas *nālā*, it was here at Curtius' *fossa praealta* that Alexander decided to secrete his select force for forcing the Hydaspes.

THE BATTLE

> The locality is the surviving portion of reality of an event that has long ago passed by ... It often restores to clearness the picture which history has preserved in half-effaced outlines.
>
> Helmuth von Moltke der Ältere

After successfully crossing the swollen, swirling Hydaspes some 150 *stadia* upriver from his main camp on the right bank, Alexander swiftly marshalled his command into marching order. He then proceeded southwards with his horsemen, leaving the infantry to follow at a comfortable footpace. In the meantime, Poros had despatched one of his sons with a force of 60 chariots (if we accept Aristoboulos' account) or 120 chariots with an escort of 2,000 horsemen (if we accept that of Ptolemaios) either to reconnoitre or, as Arrianus believes (following Ptolemaios, who claimed to have taken part in this particular engagement), to oppose Alexander's crossing upriver (*Anab*. 5.14.3–4).

In the event the Indians were too late to interrupt Alexander's fearless actions, who met this Indian force in his advance and defeated it with heavy losses in the brief spate of carnage that followed. This ended in the death of Poros' son as he vainly attempted to extricate himself. The chariots, which had been immobilized on account of being sunk deep in the muddy ooze, were captured (Arr. *Anab*. 5.15.2, Curt. 8.14.4). Those Indians who survived fled over the same ground they advanced over earlier that morning, but fewer in number and certainly less eager, and brought to Poros the news that Alexander had crossed the river and was advancing in full force. Plutarch (*Alex*. 60.4) says Alexander was 20 *stadia* (3.7km) in advance of his infantry when he fell in with the Indians under Poros' son. His rashness was justified by his success, for the rapidity of Alexander's progress had convincingly won the first round of the day.

The raja left a few elephants and an adequate force opposite the Macedonian camp to prevent Krateros from crossing in his rear, and advanced northwards with the remainder of his forces. On reaching a sandy and level position free from mud, he halted his army and drew up his troops in line of battle to await Alexander.

These arrangements are clearly described by Arrianus (*Anab*. 15.5–7). In the front line he placed his elephants at intervals of a *pléthron* (*c.* 30m, cf. Polyain. 4.3.22 who says 'fifty *podōn*' or *c.* 15m) where they would deter

THE FIRST ENCOUNTER AT THE HYDASPES (PP. 66–67)

Just before dawn, and following a tremendous thunderstorm, the Macedonian flanking force under Alexander crossed the Hydaspes employing oared boats and wooden rafts buoyed up with straw-stuffed hides. Having successfully landed unopposed on the left bank of the river, Alexander (**1**) leaves his foot soldiers to follow at their own pace, and with the *hetaîroi* (**2**) and Sakae and Dahae horse archers (**3**) he canters off to locate Poros. However, the Macedonian horsemen are soon confronted by an Indian mobile force of chariots and horsemen (**4**) led by one of Poros' sons. Alexander throws forward his horse archers and quickly follows up with the *hetaîroi*. The fair-skinned horse archers

from the windswept steppes do their ugly work by swiftly taking out the chariot crewmen. In fact, many of the chariots were to be had as easy targets for these fast-moving predators, having fallen victim to the rain-soaked ground and so rendered immobile.

With the Dahae and Sakae now hovering in the background, Alexander, at the head of the *hetaîroi*, leads them into contact against their Indian counterparts. He is riding the famed Thessalian stallion Boukephálas (**5**), a huge, black-coated creature with a massive head bearing a large white star on its brow: this will be the devoted charger's last outing. Alexander wears his idiosyncratic gilded Attic helmet in the form of a lion's head.

the Macedonian horsemen and so deal with the Macedonian infantry. In a second line behind the elephants, and hence covering the intervals between them, he stationed the bulk of his 30,000 foot warriors. The remainder he drew up on either flank of the elephant line, and finally on the extreme wings his horsemen, 2,000 on each one. In front of the horsemen were placed 300 chariots, presumably divided equally between the wings (Arr. *Anab.* 5.15.4–7).[10] Poros' tactics were going to rest on stability and security, and the comparison of his army to a city wall, with the elephants looking like towers and the foot warriors like the ramparts between them, is quite apposite (Curt. 8.14.13, Diod. 17.87.5, Polyain. 4.3.22). Poros had but the notion of a fight in parallel order, and a defensive fight at that in which mass and might would eventually win the day. The original sin of a commander is preparing to fight a battle he wants, not the battle he is likely to face. And so it was to be with Poros.

If Poros' elephants were drawn up in a single line (as Arrianus implies), the Indian battle line must have extended for about 8km across the plain. Now, if we take the calculations of Polybios (12.20–21) as a basis, the Indian foot warriors, occupying 1.8m per man, cannot have been drawn up more than eight deep. Knowing what we know about Indian foot warriors and their preference for avoiding the hazards of close-quarter combat, we would expect a greater depth than that. Georg Veith (1908: 139) may well be correct in thinking that Poros' line did not extend so far. Veith, who served in the Austro-Hungarian Army as an artillery officer, rightly emphasizes the difficulty of estimating the length of a battle line even in his day.

Whatever the actual length of the Indian battle line, Poros' dispositions were complete before Alexander decided on his order of battle, which was of course determined by the presence of the elephants in the Indian front line. He could not approach these with his horsemen or advance by the centre with his phalanx unless he was prepared to suffer heavy losses into the bargain. Consequently, with his keen eye for observation and an intuitive sense of tactical possibilities, Alexander opted to curb the elephants' freedom of movement as much as possible: his initial attack would be directed against the Indian horsemen, so relying on his superiority in that arm, which outnumbered those of the enemy by more than two-to-one. His dispositions would not be of the parallel order but the oblique order of Epameinondas, with the left refused.

As has been already indicated, the Indian horsemen were posted on the two wings of Poros' army, chariots to their front. With the greater part of his cavalry stationed on his right wing, Alexander took the offensive by despatching a thousand horse archers against the Indian left wing. The aim was to throw the foe in that part of the battlefield into confusion with a rain of arrows before swarming past them. The Sakae and Dahae, after all, were past masters in the inborn art of horse archery, a very dynamic type of shooting that relied on a combination of muscle memory, hand-eye coordination, arrow trajectory and subconscious distance calculations to the target – under the Seleukid kings they would serve as mercenaries

10 Curtius (8.13.6) and the *Metz Epitome* (54) agree with Arrianus regarding the figures for the Indian foot warriors and four-horse chariots, but only have 85 elephants. Both sources fail to mention the Indian horsemen at this point, but earlier (8.14.2) Curtius says Poros' *brother* Spitakes (cf. Arr. *Anab.* 5.18.2, an Indian *nomarchos*) was despatched with 4,000 horsemen and 100 chariots to intercept Alexander, while Polyainos (4.3.21) mentions a *grandson* of Poros as the commander of this interception force. Diodoros Siculus (17.87.2) gives 50,000 foot warriors, 3,000 horsemen, over 1,000 chariots, and 130 elephants. Plutarch (*Alex.* 62.1) mentions only 20,000 foot warriors and 2,000 horsemen.

The Hydaspes: Indian and Macedonian battle lines

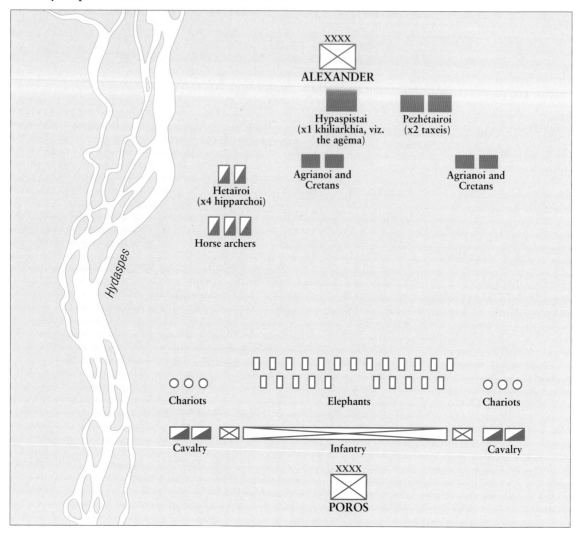

and gain a reputation as excellent *hippotoxótai*, horse archers. Mission accomplished, Alexander quickly followed up by leading a charge of the *hetaîroi*, thundering forward at speed by executing a 'flanking movement' (παρήλαυνεν/*parēlaunen*), to quote Arrianus (*Anab.* 5.16.2), so as to scupper the enemy on their left wing while they were still disorganized. True to say, outflanking and envelopment were at once a commander's greatest fear and aspiration.

Though Arrianus (*Anab.* 5.15.7) places the Indian chariots on both wings, he fails to mention them in the battle. Still, if we turn to Diodoros Siculus (17.88.1), he says practically all of the chariots on the Indian left were almost immediately *hors de combat*; presumably their crewmen were successfully shot down by the passing horse archers.

From his first-rate observation point perched as he was on his royal bull elephant, Poros reacted swiftly by ordering the horsemen on his own right wing to shift so as to reinforce the threatened left flank:

The torrent bed known as Kandar Kas, possibly Curtius' deep-cut ravine (*fossa praealta*), beside the triangular headland of Mangal Dēv, a 300m-high outcrop of the Salt Range immediately east of Jalālpur Sharif that runs towards the right bank of the Jhelum. It is conceivable that in this remote *nālā*, as the locals name such a physical feature, Alexander concealed his crossing force, hidden from view from the riverside. Even today rivers are a major obstacle to armies on the move. Yet one of Alexander's tactical specialities was the crossing of rivers in the face of the enemy, just as he had previously done at the Ister and the Jaxartes. (Jona Lending/Livius.org/CC0 1.0 Universal)

Meanwhile the Indians had brought their horsemen together from all sides and were riding parallel to Alexander and drawing out their line to match his progress. Koinos and his men, following Alexander's instructions, appeared behind them. (Arr. *Anab.* 5.17.1)

According to Arrianus, though the Greek passage is ambiguous and has provided much food for debate, the two *hipparchoi* under the command of Koinos had been despatched 'toward [or against] the right' (*Anab.* 5.16.3) with orders to attack from the rear when the Indian horsemen were occupied dealing with Alexander. Did Arrianus mean that Koinos was to move to Alexander's right or Poros' right? Curtius (8.14.17) is of little help for he merely imparts that Koinos attacked the Indian left, presumably in their rear. However, since in the previous sentence Arrianus refers to Poros' left, he is most likely referring here to Poros' right. Modern opinion varies. J.F.C. Fuller (1989: 196–97) has Alexander send Koinos to Poros' right so that his command is concealed behind a convenient depression in the ground, with orders to return in front of the Indian battle line to fall upon the flank and rear of the Indian horsemen while they are busily engaged with Alexander. A.B. Bosworth (1995: 128–29), on the other hand, rather confusingly has Koinos attack the Indian right from where he passes behind the Indian infantry to strike the Indian horsemen occupied by Alexander on the Indian left. So we have another controversy about the battle. That is to say, did the horsemen from the Indian right and the Macedonian left ride behind or in front of the Indian battle line? Then again, did the Indian horsemen ride securely behind their own line while their Macedonian counterparts crossed sagaciously to the front of it?

Whichever manoeuvre it was, and commentators have long debated upon this, following the assumption above, Koinos must have moved leftward at a fast clip so as to engage the Indian horsemen at close quarters, the preferred mode of assault of the *hetaīroi*, if they made a move to their left wing to

POROS' DILEMMA

Poros attempts to determine the axis of the main Macedonian effort, as Alexander attempts to deceive him.

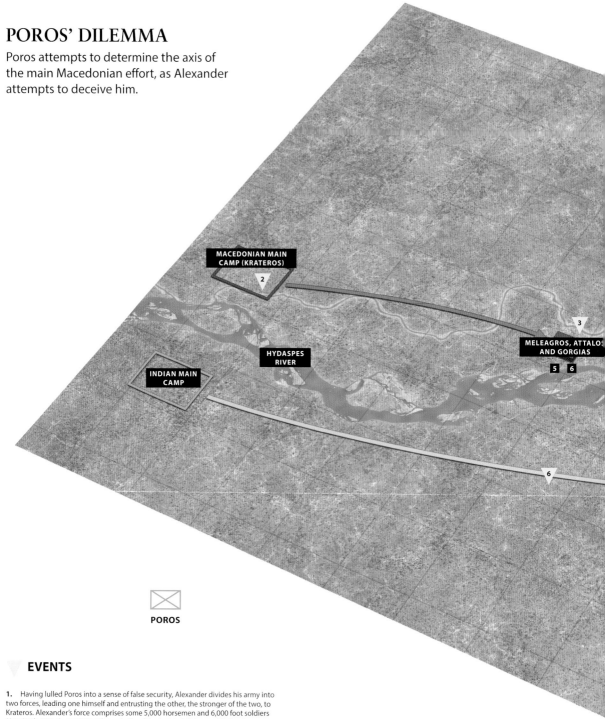

MACEDONIAN MAIN CAMP (KRATEROS)
2

3

MELEAGROS, ATTALOS AND GORGIAS
5 **6**

HYDASPES RIVER

INDIAN MAIN CAMP

6

POROS

▼ EVENTS

1. Having lulled Poros into a sense of false security, Alexander divides his army into two forces, leading one himself and entrusting the other, the stronger of the two, to Krateros. Alexander's force comprises some 5,000 horsemen and 6,000 foot soldiers (Arr. *Anab.* 5.14.1), consisting the majority of the *hetairoi*, Sakae and Dahae horse archers, *hypaspistai*, Agrianoi and Cretans, and two *taxeis* of phalangites.

2. Krateros' command, which consists of a substantial body of Macedonians along with their Indian allies, baggage train, camp followers, and so on, remains in the main camp on the right bank. It is sufficiently large to deceive Poros and hold him in his current position.

3. Meleagros, Attalos, and Gorgias are in position along the right bank north of the main camp. They act as decoys, diverting the Indians' attention from the upriver activities of Alexander.

4. Having stealthily marched some 150 *stadia* (27.8km) upriver from the main camp, Alexander reaches his pre-reconnoitred crossing point. Here he conceals his command in a deep-cut ravine hidden behind a spur running parallel to the river.

5. Under the cover of the darkness and a deluge, Alexander prepares to covertly cross the Hydaspes in order to turn Poros' formidable position downriver on the left bank.

6. Undecided at this point whether this was the main enemy effort or merely a diversionary force, Poros despatches one of his sons with a force of about 2,000 horsemen and 120 chariots to oppose Alexander's crossing.

7. Leaving the infantry to follow at their own pace, Alexander presses ahead with his horsemen to engage the Indian force.

Note: gridlines are shown at intervals of 2km (1.24 miles)

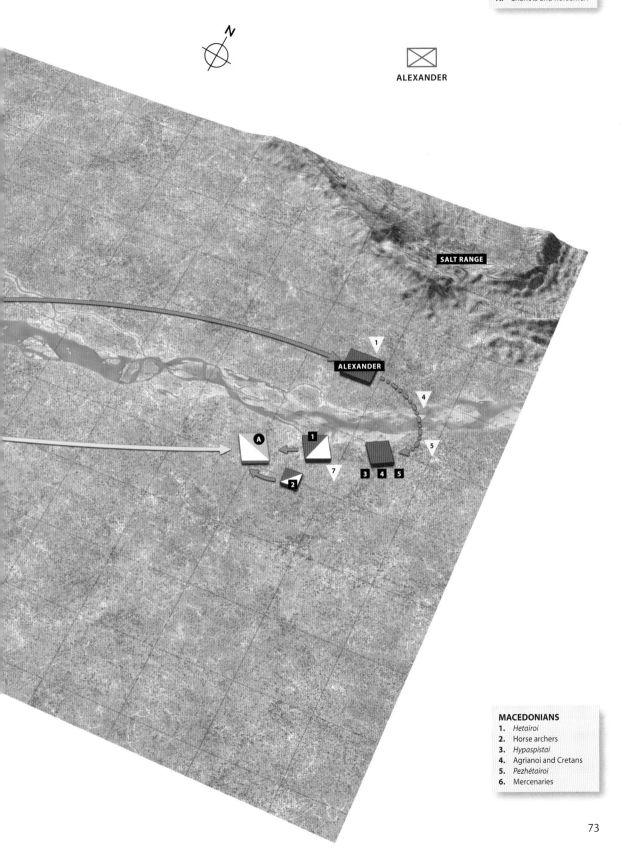

INDIANS
A. Chariots and horsemen

ALEXANDER

SALT RANGE

ALEXANDER

MACEDONIANS
1. *Hetaîroi*
2. Horse archers
3. *Hypaspistai*
4. Agrianoi and Cretans
5. *Pezhétairoi*
6. Mercenaries

Elephants, 'false capital' of the right pillar, East Gateway, Great Stūpa (No. 1), Sāñchī. At the Hydaspes, Alexander would meet a formidable opponent in Poros, but more importantly, his military genius would be challenged as never before by an unforgiving climate and a new, even larger foe, the Indian elephant (*Elephas maximus indicus*). These deeply sculptured examples at Sāñchī show the notably accurate observations of the animal's anatomy (e.g. convex line of its back, small ears, smooth trunk terminating in one 'finger', domed head, etc.), harness and decoration. Buddhist tracts (*MN* II 112, *VP* I 192) mention the fact that elephants carry a padded covering on their backs. (Amigo&oscar/ Wikimedia Commons/ CC-BY-SA-3.0)

reinforce their comrades there. Of course we have to believe that Alexander expected Poros to shift the horsemen on his right to the left. True or not, the result was to serve Alexander well, for the Indian horsemen abruptly found themselves fighting front, flank and rear. 'This tactic', says Arrianus, 'upset the Indians' formation and their presence of mind' (*Anab.* 5.17.2). When all seemed lost, they sought the shelter of the elephants. Alexander now ordered a general assault.

Poros unleashed his war elephants. These were to prove to be rather more effective than the chariots had been. Critically, however, the phalanx faithfully faced the full fury of these frightening and horrifying beasts, presumably trying to keep them at bay with their *sarissae*. Supporting the phalangites were the *hypaspistai*, preceded by a cloud of lightly armed troops, the Agrianoi and the Cretans. Much would revolve on how these infantry units would handle the Indian elephants. As Arrianus says, this 'action was like none of their previous battles; for the beasts sallied out against the *taxeis* of phalangites and ravaged them wherever they turned, despite their keeping in close formation' (*Anab.* 5.17.3). Diodoros Siculus is rather more macabre, describing how some Macedonians were 'trodden under foot, armour and all', while others were lifted up by the elephants' trunks and 'dashed back down to the ground again' or 'pierced through by the tusks' (17.88.1). Meanwhile, seeing their elephants joining the fight, the Indian horsemen took renewed heart and reengaged with their Macedonian counterparts. Their counter-attack failed.

At this point, according to Arrianus, the Agrianoi and Cretans were used to great effect against the advancing elephants, 'hurling javelins at the men mounted on them, and shooting at the beasts themselves from all sides' (*Anab.* 5.17.3). 'When the beasts were worn out,' he continues, 'and their charges were no longer vigorous – when they merely trumpeted and retired like ships backing water' (ibid. 17.7), Alexander ordered the phalanx to lock shields and push forward. In pain and panic, those elephants that survived ran amok in a grim stampede. While doing so, they spared no one, trampling down the unfortunate troops of their own side, so creating a scene of immeasurable confusion. In Curtius' dramatic retelling of this final phase of the battle, we are told:

> The elephants were finally exhausted by their wounds. They charged into their own men, mowing them down: their riders were flung to the ground and trampled to death. More terrifying than menacing, the beasts were being driven like cattle from the battlefield. (Curt. 8.14.30)

Little wonder, therefore, the Indians' cohesion was thrown into chaos and they were overrun. Indian losses are variously estimated at 12,000 or more and 23,000, of which 3,000 were horsemen, while all the chariots were destroyed and all the surviving elephants captured (Diod. 17.89.1, Arr. *Anab.* 5.18.2).

It was now long into the afternoon, and the final phase belonged to Krateros. He had been given fairly specific instructions by Alexander on how he should respond to Poros' reaction to the upriver crossing. Accordingly, he was to make open preparations to make the passage of the river, but not actually do so unless Poros' army, along with *all* his elephants, should march upstream, or he was sure Poros had been defeated (Arr. *Anab.* 5.11.3–4).

Reddish-brown sandstone railing pillar (Kolkata, Indian Museum) from the Stūpa of Bhārhut, Southwest Quadrant, dated *c.* 100 BC. This fine high relief depicts a near life-size Greek (or Indo-Greek) warrior in the rôle of *dvārapāla*, a divine door or gate guardian. He wears an *adhovāsa* garment, which reaches below the knees. Of interest too is his massive sword, broad in the blade, commonly wielded by Indian warriors. (G41m8/Wikimedia Commons/CC-BY-SA-4.0)

FIGHTING ELEPHANTS (PP. 76–77)

The Macedonians naturally dreaded Indian war elephants, which were in greater numbers and quality than anything they have yet encountered, if the 15 or so they glimpsed at Gaugamela can be counted. From their point of view, the fighting on the left bank of the Hydaspes was to become desperate and at times chaotic due to the ground made muddy by the overnight deluge, trumpeting elephants and crowded lines of opposing foot warriors.

A tremendous struggle was soon to develop as the Macedonian phalangites were tossed about or trampled under foot by the Indian elephants as they charged headlong into their formation. These Macedonian footsloggers, harsh veterans of so many hard fights, would eventually prevail in what turned out to be the hardest fought of all their pitched battles.

In this reconstruction the mahouts and warrior crew (**1**) are busily being picked off by the Agrianoi javelineers (**2**) and Cretan archers (**3**). Though extremely difficult to kill, the elephants themselves are receiving many maddening pinprick wounds (**4**). The elephants have cloth caparisons or padded mantles (**5**), which give the crew a more secure seat, held in place with twisted ropes. Some elephants have bells hung on neck ropes and elsewhere, whereas others are decorated with painted leaves and flowers (**6**). Others still have their tusks reinforced with bronze casings (**7**). Each elephant crew consists of a mahout armed with a hooked goad and occasionally with javelins too, and up to three warriors armed with bows and javelins (**8**). In the meantime, the phalangites (**9**), having recovered their wits, begin their steady advance with locked shields. Already, some of the wounded and riderless elephants are being driven back in confusion into their own foot warriors (**10**).

Similarly, the mercenary troops under three of the *taxiárchoi*, Meleagros, Attalos and Gorgias, had been positioned along the right bank north of the main camp so as to act as decoys, diverting the Indians' attention from the activities of Alexander, and ordered to cross the river when they saw the Indians already engaged in battle (ibid. 12.1, cf. Curt. 8.18.22, who gives different names). It is inferred by Arrianus that these three Macedonian commanders were with their own *taxis* of *pezhétairoi* too. Some scholars have suggested that some of these troops must have filtered across the river before the main battle was joined. However, there is no evidence that this was the case in the literary sources.

So, the ruthless pursuit of those fortunate enough to escape the mud and mayhem was taken up by Krateros' command, which had forced its way across the river by this time. He was probably joined in this vital task by the troops under Meleagros, Attalos and Gorgias. As for the Macedonian casualties, the highest figures recorded are 280 horsemen and something

Limestone frieze (Paris, Guimet musée national des arts asiatiques), detail from a life scene of the Buddha showing a female guard standing at a door with a broad-bladed sword hanging from her left side. Both fierce-looking and beautiful at the same time, she is a *pratihārīa*, a doorkeeper. Gandhāran Buddhist iconography depicts armed women guarding both Prince Siddhārtha Gautama, who became the Buddha, and his wife Yaśodharā. The intimate protectors of Indian rajas and princes, female bodyguards were trained in the use of bows, swords and shields, and were especially skilled in *mallayuddha*, literally 'wrestling combat', freestyle bare-hand fighting with no holds barred. (© Esther Carré)

ALEXANDER'S MASTERPIECE

Alexander traps Poros' army, which begins
to disintegrate.

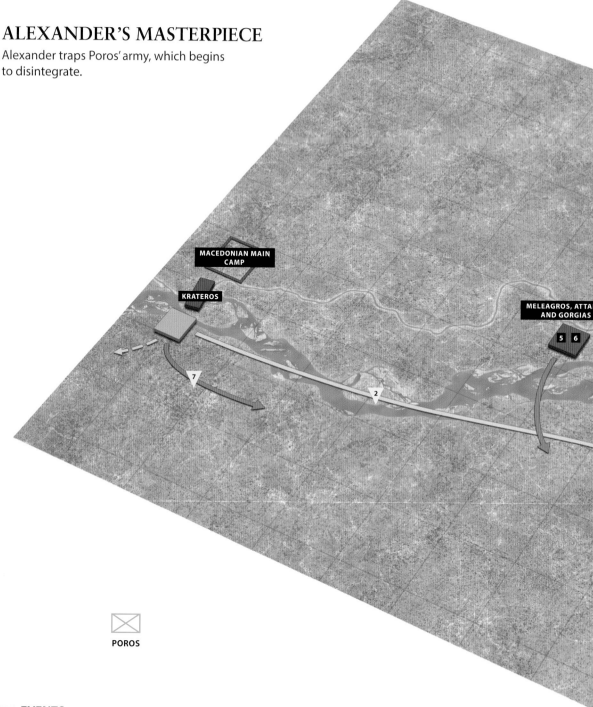

MACEDONIAN MAIN
CAMP

KRATEROS

MELEAGROS, ATTAL
AND GORGIAS

5 6

7

2

POROS

EVENTS

1. Having stolen a night passage across the storm-swollen Hydaspes and seen off the initial Indian foray against his turning force, Alexander advances along the left bank to seek Poros' main army.

2. In the meantime, leaving a force (including elephants) to keep Krateros in check, Poros commences his march towards Alexander.

3. Having found level ground free of mud and water, Poros deploys his army and awaits the arrival of Alexander.

4. Alexander, having deployed his army, launches the majority of his horsemen against Poros' left wing; the horse archers take out the Indian chariots while two *hipparchoi* of *hetairoi* led by Alexander follow close behind. At the same time, Koinos leads the other two *hipparchoi* of *hetairoi* against the Indian right.

5. Poros switches his right-wing horsemen to support those on his left wing; Koinos switches to the Indian left too. Caught between Alexander and Koinos, the Indian horsemen seek the shelter of the elephants.

6. Poros releases his elephants; the Agrianoi and Cretans skirmish against them as the Macedonian phalanx follows up behind. After a grinding and grim fight, the elephants are overcome and run amok. Poros' army begins to fall apart.

7. Krateros, having crossed the Hydaspes and dealt with Poros' holding force, advances upon Poros' rear. His command is joined by the troops under Meleagros, Attalos and Gorgias. The final phase of the battle belongs to them.

Note: gridlines are shown at intervals of 2km (1.24 miles)

ALEXANDER

INDIANS
A. Chariots and horsemen
B. Left-wing horsemen
C. Right-wing horsemen
D. Elephants
E. Foot warriors

SALT RANGE

HYDASPES RIVER

MACEDONIANS
1. *Hetaîroi*
2. Horse archers
3. *Hypaspistai*
4. Agrianoi and Cretans
5. *Pezhétairoi*
6. Mercenaries

over 700 infantry (Diod. 17.89.3, cf. Arr. *Anab.* 5.18.3). Consider, for example, that Diodoros Siculus (17.36.6) says that at Issos 300 infantry and 150 horsemen were lost, while at Gaugamela Arrianus (*Anab.* 3.15.6) says nearly 100 men and more than 1,000 horses were killed in action. In fact, a closer scrutiny of the evidence suggest that at day's end an overall figure of 4,000 might well come nearer the truth for the Hydaspes (Green 1991: 401), particularly when you consider how long and savage this battle turned out to be.

ANALYSIS

> The offensive knows what it wants, whereas the defensive is in a state of uncertainty.
>
> Helmuth von Moltke der Ältere

Whether we marvel at him or not, be it Alexander the warrior or Alexander the conqueror, the young king of Macedon held a special appeal for his army. Here was a man who excelled as a combat leader, commanding, cajoling, controlling, while inspiring his men with a spirit of deep devotion. He appealed not merely to their greed and lust, but awakened in them an indomitable sense of duty towards him, their soldier king. After years of conquest, the Macedonian army that set out for India was remarkably different from the one that had initially landed in Asia. It had become less the royal one created by Philip and more of a quasi-mercenary force with all the untamed behaviour and ungoverned ardour that eight years of war and licence had fostered. Nonetheless, at the time the army still held a deep-seated respect and admiration for the king and the Argead dynasty.

Success in any war, ancient or modern, depends primarily on three dynamics, specifically, moral qualities (e.g. courage, energy, willpower, etc.), organization and equipment, and of course leadership. Almost certainly the best of its day, the army of Alexander was a professional veteran force, battle-skilled, with tried and tested equipment and outstanding leadership, not only at the top but at all levels of command. With regards to the last dynamic, Alexander was ever dangerous, being as he was always on the move, on the attack, and he would seemingly make it all happen with absolute ease.

These observations contribute to another factor which lay in the Macedonians' favour, namely, an attacking army always retains the initiative. It can choose where and when to strike; a defender will remain uncertain as to where the main point of attack will fall. And so it was, in the all-important cavalry clash on Poros' left wing, the Indian horsemen failed in their fight against their Macedonian counterparts for two critical reasons.

First, the Macedonians were, in words of Arrianus, 'much superior … both in strength and experience' (*Anab.* 5.17.4), in other words, better trained, better disciplined and better equipped. This tactical trinity furnished them with a baked-in edge for their close-quarter combat role. What is more, with regards to their better-quality war gear, there is a supplementary corollary. Javelins were primarily designed for throwing and not thrusting; they were shorter and had lighter, slimmer shafts. The *xystón*, on the other hand, was a stout handheld weapon of greater reach. The practical, tactical and lethal advantages of *xystón* over javelin are all too clear: when fighting at close

quarters, it is best to fight with a weapon that has a longer reach than that of your opponent. For that reason alone, the Indian horsemen were at a distinct disadvantage in the hand-to-hand fighting favoured by their Macedonian counterparts. Another reason worth mentioning, on the other hand, is the fact that the Macedonian horsemen were superior not only in fighting quality but, unusually so for them, in numbers too. A double predicament for Poros was his inferiority in horsemen, who happened to be inferior as well.

Second, Alexander, who was himself a superb horseman, was a cavalry commander of outstanding, aggressive ability. His principal tactical goal was to engage the enemy in close-quarter combat at a critical point of their battle line and bring about its collapse. As at the Granīkos, Issos and Gaugamela, so here at the Hydaspes he understood the advantage of hurling his horsemen upon the enemy in sufficient numbers at the proper time so as to break through them by means of rapidity and momentum. This second reason is the important one. During the main battle it was his surgical strike that secured the day for Alexander.

The Prussian military thinker Clausewitz was to write something appropriate when he emphasized the value of the application of maximum force to achieve a decisive victory on the field of battle. At the time he was undoubtedly bearing that contemporary military genius Napoleon in mind, but Alexander, whose genius was at many points in close harmony with Napoleon's, would have equally served him as a principal exemplar. Both men in their prime had a certain talent for thinking (and acting) outside the box. Falling on the critical point with devastating dash, this was the *Leitmotiv* of Alexander's success.

Much like Clausewitz, Napoleon abhorred doctrinaire approaches to strategy. He insisted that strategy was not an exact science but a practical art of adapting means to ends. In view of that, he believed that bold departures from the rules were what made genius. Still, one rule he did not depart from was his precept to seek prompt decision by battle and in battle seek to destroy the enemy. Then again, the enemy was never an inert object, and Napoleon had the ability to process large amounts of information very rapidly, make a rapid decision under stress and then have the moral courage required to act decisively. Alexander's battlefield actions certainly indicate that he possessed this intangible quality of *coup d'oeil* too.

Alexandre et Porus (Paris, Musée du Louvre, inv. 2897), oil on canvas painted in 1673 by Charles le Brun (1619–90). This vast canvas is part of a series of four representing episodes taken from the career of the Macedonian conqueror commissioned by the painter's patron Louis XIV, who was identified closely with Alexander, as many dramatic works testify, among them Racine's *Alexandre*. Alexander has driven Poros and his army from the field, and here le Brun represents the Macedonian king showing magnanimity to the Indian raja by allowing him to retain his kingdom as the victor's gift – for Alexander had neither the means nor the desire to occupy and hold down Poros' extensive realm. The defeated Indian raja's war elephants can be seen lying dead in the background. (Tangopaso/Wikimedia Commons/Public domain)

TWO KINGS (PP. 84–85)

Poros, who has lost two sons that fateful day (Arr. *Anab.* 5.18.2), battled on bravely until the raja was wounded in the right shoulder, the only part of his upper body not protected by his armour in order to permit him to freely draw his powerful cane bow. Weak from battle fatigue, thirst and the loss of blood, Poros goaded his royal bull elephant into retreat but could not escape the field of the slain.

Here the two kings have finally come face to face in the midst of the mire and corpses, and Alexander (**1**) asks Poros (**2**) how he wishes to be treated: 'Treat me like a king', is the brief but regal reply. When pressed, Poros replies that all has been said which needs saying (Arr. *Anab.* 5.19.2). Their dialogue of course would have necessitated some linguistic gymnastics: Greek into Persian into Sanskrit and back the same way through the two interpreters (**3** and **4**), an Anatolian Greek (left) and a Persian courtier (right).

Poros was a remarkably tall man who stood around 4.5–5 cubits in height (about 2.06–2.29m). His long hair is piled into a topknot, as was the fashion. He is decked out in body armour (**5**) which no missiles could bite (Arr. *Anab.* 5.18.5), a coat of gilded and silvered iron scales. His clothing beneath is brightly coloured and patterned. An unbowed raja, Poros is not dissimilar to a heroic warrior of a long-gone past. Indeed, he appears as if he has just stepped out from one of the founding epics of Indian culture, the *Mahābhārata*.

Alexander, of short stature (perhaps a little over 1.52m) and slight physique (even by Macedonian standards), is obliged to look up so as to judge the battle-stained countenance of the man he has just overcome in mortal combat. Alexander is wearing a composite *linothōrax* with fringed *pteruges* at the shoulders and waist. The *linothōrax* is reinforced with iron scales about the waist and an iron rectangular plate on the chest, which is embossed with a design in the shape of a gorgon's head (**6**). The shoulder pieces bear a white thunderbolt motif. Underneath the king wears a pale grey long-sleeved tunic. His gilded Attic helmet (**7**), shaped like a lion's head, is being handed to a subordinate. Alexander is described as being ruddy in complexion with the right eye dark and the left one blue. Most accounts give him curly, shoulder-length flaxen hair, and fair skin. He was reportedly unable to grow a beard, and made it fashionable to go clean shaven.

In his bid to destroy (as opposed to just defeat) his enemy on the other side of the Hydaspes, Alexander performed a virtuoso tactical ruse that was to wrong-foot Poros and catch him off guard. Nonetheless, all was not lost for the raja. Though Krateros commanded a sizeable force directly opposite him across the river, Poros rightly identified Alexander as the greater threat and acted accordingly. The plan was good enough in itself, but it ought to have been devised sooner and executed with promptitude. As it was, Alexander quickly exploited his initial advantage before Poros had marched to engage him, and so set the stage for a total, albeit costly, Macedonian victory. And then there were of course the physical factors. Weather and ground weighed heavily against the Indians and their tactical doctrine at the Hydaspes. Not only did their chariots fail to deliver, but their bowstrings were rendered useless by the penetrating rain that had lashed the battlefield over the previous night.

Poros was not a conqueror; he was a regional king, a raja, rightly defending his realm.[11] As such he drew his conclusions that day, not from personal observation, but from an assumed premise. To provide perspective, he believed it was better for the enemy to attack and then defeat him with a preponderance of war elephants. So while Poros placed an excessive reliance on his signature arm to carry the day, his enemy, a more brilliant tactician, depended for his success on the skilful use of well-trained and well-equipped horsemen. These were of course the *hetaîroi* and the Thessalians, the chief striking arm of a veteran and ever-victorious army. Committing to a set confrontation on Alexander's terms played directly into his hands. At the Hydaspes, by sorry contrast, Poros was critically under-prepared to meet a man who would not take less than outright victory, paying too much attention to process, rather than outcome, and not responding quickly enough. Still, it must be stressed it was the toughest and longest pitched battle ever fought by Alexander and, as later events were to demonstrate, the nerve of his men had been severely shaken. Even so, to claim that history has been manipulated or falsified and the battle 'was a drawn game' (Prakash 1967: 78) is going too far. Supporters of this yarn are treading on weak ground.

In the final analysis, it was the adroit turning manoeuvre upriver that unhinged Poros' position on the left bank of the Hydaspes. Begun badly, the day continued worse. Dexterity was the key. The battle was essentially a general's battle, that is to say, the triumph of genius in command, not of mere bodily courage, an application of brain rather than brawn. If the Hydaspes had been a swordfight, then it would have been a duel in which one duellist was skilled with a rapier while the other was one blundering around with a broadsword. At the Hydaspes Alexander did his brilliant thing, manoeuvring the opposition's army as well as his own, making their (outdated) tactics work for him, and its outcome deprived Poros of the means and the will to fight further.

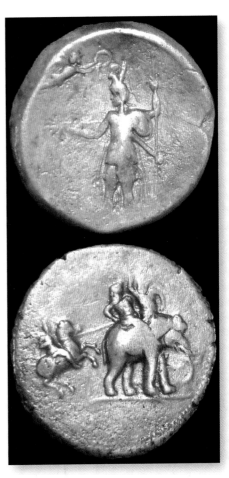

Elephant medallion (London, British Museum, inv. 1926-4-2-1), silver 'campaign medal', struck during Alexander's lifetime for veterans of the Hydaspes. The reverse depicts Alexander wearing a *chlamýs* and a Phrygian helmet with a bristled crest and two tall feathered plumes (*vide* Plut. *Alex.* 16.4: 'helmet's crest, on either side of which was fixed a plume of wonderful size and whiteness'). He is armed with a 'spear' (cropped *xystón*?) and *xíphos*. He clutches a thunderbolt (cf. thunderstorm prior to crossing the Hydaspes). He is being crowned by Nike, who hovers in front of him. On the obverse, a retreating Poros astride the royal bull elephant is confronted either by Alexander, or the 'traitor raja' Āmbhi. (PHGCOM/Wikimedia Commons/Public domain)

11 An interesting point to ponder upon: there were great rulers who ruled much of the Indian Subcontinent but never ventured out of India itself. Thus the Hindus never produced any of the world conquerors such as Alexander or Temūr-i Lang.

AFTERMATH

SEVENTH [INDIAN] PHILOSOPHER
Question: How can a man become a god?
Answer: By doing something a man cannot do.

Plut. *Alex*. 64.4

In 336 BC Alexander, aged only 20, succeeded to the throne of Macedonia on the murder of his father, Philip. Not surprisingly, as the son was the main beneficiary of his father's death, there were insinuations that he had directed the dagger of the assassin (Plut. *Alex*. 10.6–7). True or not, Alexander's position was far from secure at this point, and his companions gathered around him and occupied the palace at Aigai, already armed and all set for battle (Arr. *Anab*. 1.25.2). It was a dangerous throne as his claim to it was likely to be challenged and an attempt on his life was a distinct possibility given the dynastic troubles of Philip's last year. With an in-house free-for-all looming large in Macedonia, subject peoples to the north and south of the kingdom deemed the occasion as the perfect moment to throw off the Macedonian yoke.

Close to 13 years later Alexander, still not 33 years old, succumbed to fever (many said poison removed him) in the humid lowlands of Babylon, in the heart of the now defunct Persian empire. Not only had he overcome his difficulties at home – most of the extended Argead family were quickly liquidated – defeated the neighbouring Illyrians and Paionians, flattened Thebes – 20,000 enslaved, 6,000 executed – and established himself as the acknowledged leader of the Greek world (Sparta notwithstanding),[12] but even the might of Persia had fallen before him. Having led his army on a conquering trek of some 17,700km in eight years to the very edge of the known world, Alexander held sway over a polyglot empire that covered some 3.2 million km^2. Here was a man who was splendidly lacking in the understanding of knowing when to stop.

Alexander finally did stop his conquest at the behest of his worn-out soldiers; according to Plutarch, 'their struggle with Poros blunted their courage and stayed their further advance into India' (*Alex*. 62.1). It is clear that, after eight years of marching and conquering, there was a widespread sense of exhaustion across Alexander's army. Strabo (15.1.27) comments that the men suffered most of all from the drenching deluge, which had fallen incessantly since they left the Hydaspes at the start of the monsoon season

---

12   One anecdote tells that Philip sent a message to the Spartans saying, 'If I enter Lakonia, I will level Sparta to the ground'. The reply from the Spartans was only one word, 'If' (Plut. *Mor*. 511a).

Inner face, second panel of the left pillar, North Gateway, Great Stūpa (No. 1), Sāñchī. This is the best preserved of all the gateways, and was the second to be erected. The numerous carved panels depict various event of the life of the Buddha. In this one we witness a raja and his royal cortège leaving Rājagṛiha (modern Rajgir), the first capital of the kingdom of Magadha, which would eventually evolve into the Mauryan empire (321–185 BC). The exhausted army of Alexander approached the western reaches of Magadha, where it mutinied at the Hyphasis (Beās) River and refused to march further east, fearful of meeting another formidable Indian army. The raja rides in a two-horse chariot. The chariot cab is of light construction – leather on a wicker or wooden framework – high at the front and open at the rear. It is fixed centrally on a wooden axle fastened by strps of ox hide. Secured to the axle by lynch pins, the iron-shod wheels are small with 16 spokes per wheel. (Bernard Gagnon/Wikimedia Commons/ CC-BY-SA-3.0)

(Diod. 17.94.3), saturating them and the land alike and making mud the only certainty. The recent affair before the walls of Sangala had resulted in more than 1,200 wounded, including Lysimakhos (Arr. *Anab.* 5.24.5). Even a competent commander knows when not to push his men beyond their capability and level of motivation, and it is not to Alexander's credit that on this occasion he had failed to appraise correctly their low morale and physical condition. The truth was the blooded veterans of the Hydaspes were weary, wet, dispirited, and a long way from home. Faced with their king's insatiable urge for more they saw little hope of their own survival or their return, and so mutinied (ibid. 25.2, 27.6, Curt. 9.2.6–11, 3.1).

Alexander, especially in the last couple of years of his life, looked less like the Alexander of the past. The near-paranoid king plainly had developed a dysfunctional relationship with his army whereby he only saw obedient collaborators who fell in line or enemies who raised their heads and had to be crushed. Yet even autocrats have whispers in their ears, sometimes an advisor wiser than they are, sometimes an advisor whose cast of mind has rendered him or her briefly indispensable. All need someone who in a moment of crisis can quietly tell them, 'You are misguided'. Reputedly on this occasion that someone was Koinos, who recalled Alexander to his honour-bound duty to his men and to the responsibilities of being the king of the Macedonians:

The Beās viewed from the hill station of Kullu, Himachal Pradesh, India. The Hyphasis to the Greeks, somewhere on its right bank, north of Gurdāspur and south of Pathancot, the army of Alexander made its easternmost camp. It was here that the great conqueror faced a feuding staff and febrile soldiery. Eight years away from home and weary of constant slogging through the ceaseless monsoon, which deteriorated equipment, bodies and morale, the hard-tried army refused to go a step further. Reminiscent of Achilles withdrawing from the fighting beneath the walls of Troy because his honour had been slighted, Alexander shut himself away in his tent for three days, fuming and raging before finally relenting. He had undertaken what could not be accomplished – the subjugation of the Indian Subcontinent. To preserve his claim of divine origins, prior to quitting the river he ordered the army to construct a dozen colossal memorial altars built of squared stone (Arr. *Anab.* 5.29.1). The altars, which became a standard feature of mediaeval world maps but are long lost, were dedicated to the gods to mark the limit of his great expedition. The elder Pliny (6.21) stands alone in placing these altars on the left bank of the river. (Jupitus Smart/Wikimedia Commons/ CC-BY-SA-4.0)

'Nothing is as honourable as the self-restraint in the midst of good fortune' (Arr. *Anab.* 5.27.9). In the eyes of Koinos, Alexander was at a crossroads seemingly not of his own choosing, and almost certainly not of his liking. All power corrupts the more absolutely it grows. Now corruption is a slippery concept, but it does sometimes suggest something past its peak and beginning to decay.

With the end of Alexander's odyssey on account of his untimely demise, the forces of disintegration were to prove too strong to be permanently surmounted. Without the unifying hand and a common enemy all the petty jealousies and divisions amongst Alexander's generals were suddenly exposed as they started to squabble about his body at Babylon. The vastness of his empire born from conquest and the selfish ambitions of these generals meant Alexander's success was partial and temporary. Yet his conquests shaped the world stage not only for the generals-turned-kings that struggled in vain to take his place, but later for the Romans too in their attempts to follow the footsteps of that great ghost. Still, the fact remains that Alexander was a man it was impossible to replicate because he was a legend as well as himself. On the one hand, like world conquerors that came before and after him, Alexander possessed an overriding autocratic devotion to triumph and battle-fuelled glory. On the other hand, however, Alexander was unique. Here was a personality to make the difficult easy and the impossible possible. His mind's eye was infinite.

The image of the legendary Macedonian conqueror has inspired ambitious military men to emulate his achievements for centuries. Of these Iulius Caesar stands apart in having taught himself in middle life how to successfully wage war, his Gallic campaigns serving as a practical school of warfare in which he could learn his brutal trade. Earlier in his life, while serving as *quaestor* in Hispania Ulterior (69 BC), Caesar had visited a shrine dedicated to Herakles in Gades. It was there, according to Suetonius, that an envious Caesar gazed upon Alexander's statue and sighed that at his age 'Alexander had already conquered the world' (*Iul.* 7.1). Alexander is not the first world conqueror of whom such things could be said. Kyros the Great was the founder of the gigantic empire Alexander overthrew, and if greatness is measured by the longevity of one's empire, Kyros was indeed greater – for his empire survived him by two centuries. Alexander's, on the other hand, did not make it beyond his premature death. But none have been so thrillingly defined by the one great adventure that came to make his name, a name that still retains a living fascination to this day.

Alexander departed the world stage as quickly as he entered it, and it should come of no surprise that his memory is obfuscated by hate, hype and hero-worship. Consider, for example, Saint Augustine (*City of God* 4.4), who vilifies Alexander as a murderer and a plunderer. Similarly, Dante (*Inferno* 12.107) places Alexander in the seventh circle of Hell in the company of tyrants, murderers and thieves, whilst his near-contemporary Petrarch celebrates Alexander, who 'from Pella to India / swiftly won diverse lands' (*Trionfo della fama* II.11–12). Historians are equally divided.

On the eve of campaign Alexander appeared in the dream of the great imitator of the Macedonian monarch, Pyrrhos of Epeiros, who asked what aid the restless dead king could promise for the morrow. '"My name itself will give it," said the king' (Plut. *Pyrr.* 11.2). And so it came to be.

ABBREVIATIONS

Ael.	Aelianus	
	NA	*De natura animalium*
	Takt.	*Taktiká*
AHB	*Ancient History Bulletin*	
AJA	*American Journal of Archaeology*	
Aisch.	Aischines	
AM	*Athenische Mitteilungen*	
AncW	*Ancient World*	
Archil.	Archilochos	
Arr.	Arrianus	
	Anab.	*Anabasis Alexandri*
	Ind.	*Indikē*
	Takt.	*Téchne Taktiké*
AS	*Arthaśāstra*	
Askl.	Asklepiodotos	
	Taktiká	
Athēn.	Athēnaios *Deipnosophistae* (*Banquet of the Learned*)	
Austin	M.M. Austin, *The Hellenistic World from Alexander to the Roman Conquest: A Selection of Ancient Sources in Translation* (Cambridge, 1981)	
BCH	*Bulletin de Correspondance Hellénique*	
Curt.	Curtius	
	Historiae Alexandri Magni Macedonis	
DCV	*De capitis vulneribus* (*On Head Wounds*)	
Dem.	Demosthenes	
Diod.	Diodoros Siculus	
DN	*Dīgha Nikāya*	
FGrHist	F. Jacoby, *Die Fragmente der griechischen Historiker* (Leiden, 2004)	
Frontin.	Frontinus	
	Strategemata	
GJ	*Geographical Journal*	
Gk.	Greek	
G&R	*Greece and Rome*	
Harding	P. Harding, *Translated Documents of Greece and Rome 2: From the End of the Peloponnesian War to the Battle of Ipsus* (Cambridge, 1985)	

Hdt.	Herodotos	
	Hist.	*Historia*
IG	*Inscriptiones Graecae* (Berlin, 1923–)	
Il.	*Iliad*	
IS	*Iranian Studies*	
JHS	*Journal of Hellenic Studies*	
JNAA	*Journal of the Numismatic Association of Australia*	
Just.	Justinus	
	Epitome (of Cnaeus Pompeius Trogus)	
L.	Latin	
Mbh	*Mahābhārata*	
Metz Epit.	*Metz Epitome*	
MN	*Majjhima Nikāya*	
OP	Old Persian	
Paus.	Pausanias	
Polyain.	Polyainos	
	Strategemata	
Polyb.	Polybios	
Plin.	Pliny (the Elder)	
	Naturalis historia	
Plut.	Plutarch	
	Alex.	*Alexander*
	Dem.	*Demosthenes*
	Mor.	*Moralia*
	Pyrr.	*Pyrrhos*
ṚV	*Ṛgveda*	
San.	Sanskrit	
Strab.	Strabo	
	Geographia	
Suet.	Suetonius	
	Iul.	*Divus Iulius*
Theophr.	Theophrastos *Historia plantarum* (*Enquiry into Plants*)	
Thuc.	Thucydides	
VP	*Vinaya Piṭaka*	
Xen.	Xenophon	
	Anab.	*Anabasis*
	Hell.	*Hellenika* ('History of My Times')
	PH	*Perì hippikēs* ('Art of Horsemanship')

BIBLIOGRAPHY

Andronikos, M., *Vergina: The Royal Tombs and the Ancient City*, Athens: Ekdotike Athenon, 1984

Bloedow, E., 'Alexander the Great at the Hydaspes River in 326 BC', *Athenaeum*, 92/2, 2008, pp. 499–534

Bose, P., *Alexander the Great's Art of Strategy*, London: Profile Books, 2003/2004

Bosworth, A.B., *Conquest and Empire: The Reign of Alexander the Great*, Cambridge: Cambridge University Press, 1988/1995

Bosworth, A.B., *Alexander in the East: The Tragedy of Triumph*, Oxford: Oxford University Press, 1996

Bosworth, A.B. and Baynham, E.J. (eds.), *Alexander the Great in Fact and Fiction*, Oxford: Oxford University Press, 2000

Briant, P., *Alexandre le Grand*, Paris: Presse Universitaires de France, (9th edition) 2019

Brunt, P.A., 'Alexander's Macedonian cavalry', *Journal of Hellenic Studies*, 83, 1963, pp. 27–46

Brunt, P.A., 'The aims of Alexander', *Greece and Rome*, 12, 1965, pp. 205–15

Buckler, J., *Philip II and the Sacred War*, Cambridge, MA: Harvard University Press, 1989

Burn, A.R., 'The generalship of Alexander the Great', *Greece and Rome*, 12, 1965, pp. 140–54

Carney, E.D. and Ogden, D. (eds.), *Philip II and Alexander the Great: Father and Son, Lives and Afterlives*, Oxford: Oxford University Press, 2010

Cartledge, P., *Alexander the Great: The Hunt for a New Past*, London: Macmillan, 2004

Cawkwell, G.L., *Philip of Macedon*, London: Faber & Faber, 1978

Chakravarti, P.C., *The Art of War in Ancient India*, Delhi: Kalpaz Publications, 1941/2017

Connolly, P., 'Experiments with the *sarissa* – the Macedonian pike and cavalry lance: a functional view', *Journal of Roman Military Equipment Studies*, 11, 2000, pp. 103–12

Devine, A.M., 'The battle of the Hydaspes: a tactical and source-critical study', *Ancient World*, 16, 1987, pp. 91–113

Ellis, J.R., *Philip II and Macedonian Imperialism*, Princeton, NJ: Princeton University Press, 1976

Engels, D.W., *Alexander the Great and the Logistics of the Macedonian Army*, Berkeley and Los Angeles, CA: University of California Press, 1978

Erskine, A., 'The πεζέταιροι of Philip II and Alexander III', *Historia*, 38/4, 1989, pp. 385–94

Fildes, A. and Fletcher, J., *Alexander the Great: Son of the Gods*, London: Duncan Baird Publishers, 2001

Fuller, J.F.C., *The Generalship of Alexander the Great*, New York, NY: Da Capo Press, 1958/1989

Gaebel, R.E., *Cavalry Operations in the Greek World*, Norman, OK: University of Oklahoma Press, 2002

Goukowsky, P., 'Le roi Pôros, son elephant et quelques autres (en marge de Diodore xvii, 88, 6)', *Bulletin de Correspondance Hellénique*, 96, 1972, pp. 473–502

Goukowsky, P., *Essai sur les origines du mythe d'Alexandre, I: Les Origines*, Nancy: Université de Nancy, 1978

Goyal, S.R., *Kauṭilya and Megasthenes*, Delhi: Kusumanjali Prakashan, 1985

Green, P., *Alexander of Macedon, 356–323 BC: A Historical Biography*, Berkeley and Los Angeles, CA: University of California Press, (2nd edition) 1974/1991

Griffith, G.T. (ed.), *Alexander the Great: The Main Problems*, Cambridge: Heffer, 1966

Habicht, M.E., Chugg, A.M., Varotto, E. and Galassi, F.M., 'The so-called Porus medallions of Alexander the Great', *Journal of the Numismatic Association of Australia*, 29, 2018–2019, pp. 24–50

Hamilton, J.R., 'The cavalry battle at the Hydaspes', *Journal of Hellenic Studies*, 76, 1956, pp. 26–31

Hamilton, J.R., *Alexander the Great*, Pittsburgh, PA: University of Pittsburgh Press, 1973

Hammond, N.G.L., *Alexander the Great: King, Commander and Statesman*, Bristol: Bristol University Press, (2nd edition) 1989

Hammond, N.G.L., *Philip of Macedon*, Baltimore, MD: Johns Hopkins University Press, 1994

Hammond, N.G.L., *The Genius of Alexander the Great*, Chapel Hill, NC: University of North Carolina Press, 1997

Hammond, N.G.L. and Griffith, G.T., *A History of Macedonia*, 2 vols, Oxford: Oxford University Press, 1972–79

Hatzopoulos, M.B. and Loukopoulos, L.D. (eds.), *Philip of Macedon*, Athens: Ekdotike Athenon, 1980

Holt, F.L., *Alexander the Great and the Mystery of the Elephant Medallions*, Berkeley and Los Angeles, CA: University of California Press, 2003

Howe, T., 'Plutarch, Arrian and the Hydaspes: a historiographical approach', in C. Bearzot and F. Landucci (eds.), *Alexander's Legacy*, Roma: «L'Erma» di Bretschneider, 2016, pp. 25–39

Kartunen, K, *India and the Hellenistic World*, Helsinki: Finnish Oriental Society, 1997

Lane Fox, R., *Alexander the Great*, London: Penguin Books, 1973/1986

Lloyd, J.G., *Alexander the Great: Selections from Arrian*, Cambridge: Cambridge University Press, 1981

Lonsdale, D.L., *Alexander Killer of Men: Alexander the Great and the Macedonian Art of War*, London: Constable, 2004

Markle, M.M., 'The Macedonian *sarissa*, spear, and related armor', *American Journal of Archaeology*, 81/3, 1977, pp. 323–39

Marshall, J., *A Guide to Sāñchī*, Calcutta: Superintendent Government Printing, 1918

Marshall, J. and Foucher, A., *The Monuments of Sāñchī*, 3 vols, Delhi: Swati Publications, 1983

M'Crindle, J.W., *The Invasion of India by Alexander the Great*, London: Archibald Constable and Company, (2nd edition) 1896

Moorkerji, R.K., *Chandragupta Maurya and his Times*, Delhi: Motilal Banarsidass Publishers, (3rd edition) 1960

Mortani, K. and Zahir, M., 'Alexander the Great at Aornos (Mount Pir-Sar), District Shangla, Khyber Pakhtunkhwa Province, Pākistān: report on historical and archaeological field investigations (2017–2018)', *Pakistan Heritage*, 10, 2018, pp. 161–78

Mossé, C., *Alexandre: La destinée d'un mythe*, Paris: Éditions Payot & Rivages, 2001

Norozi, N., 'The «Metal Army» of Alexander in the war against the Indian king Porus in three Persian Alexander books (tenth–fourteenth centuries)', *Iranian Studies*, 52/5–6, 2019, pp. 903–22

Ogden, D., *Alexander the Great: Myth, Genesis and Sexuality*, Exeter: Exeter University Press, 2011

Ojha, K.C., *The History of Foreign Rule in Ancient India*, Allahabad: Gyan Prakashan, 1968

Oppen de Ruiter, B.F., van, 'Monsters of military might: elephants in Hellenistic history and art', *Arts*, 8/4, 2019, pp. 1–37

Prag, A.J.N.W., Musgrave, J.H. and Neave, R.A.H., 'The skull from Tomb II at Vergina: king Philip II of Macedon', *Journal of Hellenic Studies*, 104, 1984, pp. 60–78

Prag, A.J.N.W., 'Reconstructing King Philip II: the "nice" version', *American Journal of Archaeology*, 94/2, 1990, pp. 237–47

Prakash, B., *History of Poros*, Patiala: Punjabi University Press, 1967 (reprinted as *Poros the Great*, Lahore: Gautam Publishers, 1994)

Ramachandra Dikshitar, V.R., *War in Ancient India*, Madras: Macmillan and Co., 1944

Renault, M., *The Nature of Alexander*, London: Penguin Books, 1975/1983

Rice, E.E., *Alexander the Great*, Stroud: Sutton Publishing, 1997/2004

Riginos Swift, A., 'The wounding of Philip II of Macedon: fact and fabrication', *Journal of Hellenic Studies*, 114, 1994, pp. 103–19

Roisman, J. (ed.), *Brill's Companion to Alexander the Great*, Leiden: E.J. Brill, 2003

Schreider, H. and Schreider, F., 'In the Footsteps of Alexander the Great', *National Geographic*, 133/1, 1968, pp. 1–66

Singh, S.D., *Ancient Indian Warfare with Special Reference to the Vedic Period*, Leiden: E.J. Brill, 1965

Sotiriades, G., 'Das Schlachtfeld von Charonea', *Athenische Mitteilungen*, 28, 1903, pp. 301–30

Stein, M.A., *On Alexander's Track to the Indus*, London: Macmillan and Co., 1929

Stein, M.A., 'The site of Alexander's passage of the Hydaspes and the battle with Poros', *Geographical Journal*, 80/1, 1932, pp. 31–46

Stein, M.A., 'On Alexander's campaigns in the Panjāb', in M.A. Stein, *Archaeological Reconnaissance in North-Western India and South-Eastern Īrān*, Vol. 1, London: Macmillan and Co., 1937, pp. 1–44

Stoneman, R. (ed.), *Legends of Alexander the Great*, London: J.M. Dent, 1994

Stoneman, R., *Alexander the Great: A Life in Legend*, New Haven, CT: Yale University Press, 2008

Tarn, W.W., *Alexander the Great*, 2 Vols, Cambridge: Cambridge University Press, 1948

Tarn, W.W., *The Greeks in Baktria and India*, Chicago Ridge, IL: Ares Publishers, (3rd revised edition) 1997

Thapliyal, U.P., *Warfare in Ancient India: Organizational and Operational Dimensions*, New Delhi: Monohar Publishers, 2010

Veith, G., 'Die Kavalleriekampf am Hydaspes', *Klio*, 8, 1908, pp. 131–53

Wickramasinghe, C.S.M, 'The Indian invasion of Alexander and the emergence of hybrid cultures', *Indian Historical Review*, 48/1, 2021, pp. 69–91

Witzel, M., 'The development of the Vedic canon and its schools: the social and political milieu', in M. Witzel (ed.), *Inside the Texts, Beyond the Texts*, Cambridge, MA: Harvard University Press, 1997, pp. 257–348

Wood, M., *In the Footsteps of Alexander the Great*, London: BBC Books, 1997

Worthington, I., *Alexander the Great: Man and God*, Harlow: Pearson Education, 2004

INDEX